WITHDRAWN

TODAY'S WRITERS
AND THEIR WORKS

HARUKI MURAKAMI

TODAY'S WRITERS
AND THEIR WORKS

HARUKI MURAKAMI

Mark Mussari

Marshall Cavendish
Benchmark
New York

This publication represents the opinions and views of the author based on Mark Mussari's
personal experience, knowledge, and research. The information in this book serves as a general
guide only. The author and publisher have used their best efforts in preparing this book and
disclaim liability rising directly and indirectly from the use and application of this book.
Other Marshall Cavendish Offices:

Marshall Cavendish International (Asia) Private Limited, 1 New Industrial Road, Singapore
536196 • Marshall Cavendish International (Thailand) Co Ltd. 253 Asoke, 12th Flr,
Sukhumvit 21 Road, Klongtoey Nua, Wattana, Bangkok 10110, Thailand •
Marshall Cavendish (Malaysia) Sdn Bhd, Times Subang, Lot 46, Subang Hi-Tech
Industrial Park, Batu Tiga, 40000 Shah Alam, Selangor Darul Ehsan, Malaysia
Marshall Cavendish is a trademark of Times Publishing Limited
All websites were available and accurate when this book was sent to press.

Library of Congress Cataloging-in-Publication Data
Mussari, Mark. • Haruki Murakami / by Mark Mussari.
p. cm. — (Today's writers and their works) • Includes filmography. • Includes
bibliographical references. • ISBN 978-0-7614-4124-3 • 1. Murakami, Haruki, 1949- •
2. Authors, Japanese—20th century—Biography. • I. Title. • PL856.U673Z8335 2010
895.6'35—dc22 • [B] • 2009028906

Publisher: Michelle Bisson • Art Director: Anahid Hamparian
Series Designer: Alicia Mikles • Photo research by Lindsay Aveilhe

The photographs in this book are used by permission and through the courtesy of:
Marion Ettlinger, www.marionettlinger.com: cover; Elena Seibert: 6; Robert Holmes/Corbis:
13; Filip Singer/epa/Corbis: 14; Reuters: 18; Louis K. Meisel Gallery, Inc./Corbis: 23; 1989,
from A Wild Sheep Chase, by Haruki Murakami, translated by Alfred Birnbaum. Used by
permission of Alfred A. Knopf, a division of Random House, Inc.: 25; Courtesy of the artist.
Collection of the Japanese Cultural and Community Center, Seattle, Washington: 28; AP
Images: 39 (top); Michael S. Yamashita/Corbis: 39 (bottom); Blank Archives/Getty Images:
42; "Tokyo Night" by Wolfram Ruoff. Courtesy of Sous Les Etoiles Gallery: 45 (top); Greg
Elms/Lonely Planet Images/Corbis: 45 (bottom); "Love Monster Come To Me Again" by Aiko
Nakagawa, Mixmedia on Canvas, 2008: 46; 1997, from The Wind-Up Bird Chronicle, by Haruki
Murakami. Used by permission of Alfred A. Knopf, a division of Random House, Inc.: 48;
"Song Bird" by Masakatsu Kondo. Courtesy of the artist: 53; Hulton Archive/Getty Images:
60; 2005, from Kafka on the Shore, by Haruki Murakami, translated by Philip Gabriel. Used by
permission of Alfred A. Knopf, a division of Random House, Inc.: 72; Michael Brosilow: 84, 90.

Printed in Malaysia (T)
135642

CONTENTS

Japanese author Haruki Murakami has become famous worldwide for his fiction writing, which is simultaneously dreamlike and edgy.

INTRODUCTION

JAPANESE AUTHOR HARUKI MURAKAMI has achieved worldwide success and earned the respect of both critics and the reading public. His dreamlike novels and short stories have been translated into more than forty languages. Murakami's eclectic writing style reflects his broad interests, especially his love for jazz music and his knowledge of popular culture. Still, his undeniable appeal stems from three major accomplishments: the elegance of his lively writing, the depth of his psychological insights, and the entertaining voice of his narrators.

Murakami seemed to develop almost reluctantly as a writer. By his own admission he was neither a stellar student nor particularly interested in the literary culture of his native land. However, he grew up reading American fiction, and once he learned English he began to love reading in that language. Even after majoring in drama at college, Murakami decided not to become a writer but to open a jazz club. Yet, in time he felt the urge to write and published his first novel, *Hear the Wind Sing,* in 1979.

The first of his novels to be translated for the English-speaking world was *A Wild Sheep Chase,* which Murakami regards as his actual debut. With this book, heavily influenced by the author's love for the hard-boiled American author Raymond Chandler, Murakami established his international reputation. Since then, he has won numerous awards and amassed fans all over the world with his highly imaginative works, including *Norwegian Wood*, *The Wind-Up Bird Chronicle*, and *Kafka on the Shore*. In 2008, Murakami published his first memoir: *What I Talk About When I Talk About Running*.

1

LIFE AND TIMES

IN 1978 HARUKI MURAKAMI had a strange epiphany while attending a baseball game. He was sitting in the outfield stands and drinking beer during the opening game of his favorite Japanese team, the Yakult Swallows. Murakami was so impressed with the performance of an American-born batter that he felt a surge of inspiration to write a novel. "And it was at that exact moment that a thought struck me: *You know what? I could try writing a novel*," he has explained. The novel that poured out of Murakami was merely the first step in the most popular literary career ever achieved by a Japanese author. The young man who loved American culture was about to revolutionize Japanese literature and become one of the world's most admired novelists.

Youthful Endeavors

Haruki Murakami was born January 12, 1949, in Kyoto, Japan's old imperial capital. His father, Chiaki, was the son of a Buddhist priest. His mother, Miyuki, grew up in a merchant's family from Osaka. While Murakami was a small child his family moved to a number of suburbs near Kobe, and he has recalled a happy childhood of walking the hills and swimming with friends at local beaches. His parents, who met while they were both teaching Japanese literature, filled the home of their only child with many cultural traditions.

Although Murakami became an avid reader in this literary household, his tastes began to run counter to his parents' more traditional preferences. "My parents were always talking about Japanese literature," he once told a reporter, "and I hated it." Instead, he preferred to read world literature, including Russian authors like Fyodor Dostoevsky and British writers like Charles Dickens. As a teenager Murakami also read paperbacks by such popular American writers as Kurt Vonnegut, F. Scott Fitzgerald, and Truman Capote.

Once he learned English, Murakami began to devour books by American mystery writers. The hard-boiled detective writer Raymond Chandler became a favorite of the Japanese youth, who has said he loved the experience of being moved by literature written in another language.

Murakami's literary interests did not translate into good grades as a student. He refused to study and has said he was even beaten by some of his middle-school teachers. Growing up in Japan after World War II, Murakami fell in love with American culture. "I was very influenced by its music, television shows, cars, clothes, everything," he told Jay McInerney in an interview for the *New York Times*.

In 1964, at the age of fifteen, Murakami made another major discovery in his life when he experienced his first jazz concert. As a birthday present he received a ticket to see the American drummer Art Blakey. "That was the first time I really listened to jazz, and it bowled me over," he has recalled. "I never heard such amazing music, and I was hooked." He began to skip lunch to save money to buy jazz records. The rhythms of jazz would eventually become a driving force in Murakami's writing.

After high school Murakami attended Waseda University in Tokyo and majored in drama studies. "I didn't study in high school," he has admitted, "but I *really* didn't study in college." Although he found little satisfaction in the drama program, Murakami did spend a lot of time reading screenplays in the college's library. He tried to write his own screenplays but soon abandoned the effort, partly because he did not want to have to work with other people to produce a film. Early on he recognized himself as an individualist who was resistant to joining groups. While avoiding studying at Waseda, Murakami met his future wife, Yoko Takahashi, in 1968.

At this time many of Japan's universities experienced great student unrest and demonstrations. Although he sympathized with the students' concerns, Murakami's tendency to remain a loner made him uncomfortable taking part in their activities. Later he crafted a biting satire of these student radicals in his megahit novel *Norwegian Wood*. Murakami was repelled by any form of groupthink; this trait would also surface in many of his fictional protagonists.

Jazz and Cats

Murakami and Yoko married in 1971, and he interrupted his studies as the young couple took jobs in record shops and coffee houses to make ends meet. In 1974 Murakami fulfilled an early dream—to own a jazz club. With the help of a loan from family and friends, the couple purchased a basement location in a Tokyo suburb: the room functioned as a coffeehouse by day and a jazz bar at night. They named the bar Peter Cat, after one of Murakami's former pets. While managing the club Murakami read as often as he could and spent his nights observing "real live human beings." In 1975, at the age of twenty-six, Murakami finally finished his undergraduate degree; Yoko had graduated on time in 1972.

In 1977 Murakami and Yoko moved Peter Cat to a downtown Tokyo location, where they filled the bar with images of cats, including John Tenniel's illustration of the Cheshire Cat from *Alice in Wonderland*. The bar survived for four more years until a flash of enlightenment compelled Murakami to turn his attention full-time toward writing. Yet, both his love for cats and the importance of his bar would play significant roles in his literary endeavors.

Literary Beginnings

In 1978, at the age of twenty-nine, Murakami experienced a revelation while attending a baseball game. Inspired by the excellent performance of a batter, he decided he had to write a novel. On the way home from the game he bought

Cats have played an important role in Murakami's life and fiction. In Japanese culture, ceramic cats are placed in front of people's homes and businesses to ensure good fortune.

Murakami met his wife, Yoko, while they were college students, and she has supported him in all of his endeavors, from opening a jazz bar to marathon running to quitting his job to write full time—all en route to his winning the 2006 Franz Kafka Prize and other honors.

a fountain pen and paper, and—writing mostly in the wee hours of the night after the bar had closed—he began to compose his first book. He has admitted to being strongly influenced by two American authors known for their social satire: Kurt Vonnegut (1922–2007) and Richard Brautigan (1935–1984).

Six months later, in 1979, Murakami finished his first novel, *Hear the Wind Sing*, and submitted it to *Gunzo Magazine*'s New Writer's Award. To his amazement, it won. In an interview with *Publisher's Weekly,* he described his first book as "a young man, things-are-changing kind of novel" set in "the age of the counterculture" in 1970.

Early Novels

Hear the Wind Sing

With *Hear the Wind Sing* Murakami established an unnamed narrator who would appear in three more novels. He set his story in the summer of 1970, when a twenty-one-year-old biology major has come home for vacation. The narrator's mind almost seems to rummage through his memories, and the novel's wandering narrative structure follows suit. As Jay Rubin points out in his entry on Murakami in the *Dictionary of Literary Biography*: "Murakami has said he did not write the events of the narrative in chronological order but 'shot' each scene separately and later strung these events together."

To refer to the "I" of the narrator, Murakami used an

informal Japanese word usually reserved for young men: *boku*. Most Japanese first-person narratives employed a more formal word for "I." With the use of this informal pronoun, along with the narrator's detached tone and his frequent references to pop culture, Murakami had created a new voice in Japanese literature. Early in the novel the narrator recalls closing his grandmother's eyelids the night she died. In a parallel fashion, Murakami appeared to be closing the door on the ultratraditional approach to literature that had dominated the arts in Japan.

Early Themes and Motifs

While *Hear the Wind Sing* represents an early, unpolished work by a budding author, fans of Murakami's writing will recognize certain themes and motifs that have come to characterize much of his writing. The narrator reveals an aimless quality in his response to life, and much of the plot seems to take place in the dreamlike landscape of memory. He is actually twenty-nine years old, looking back on the events of that summer and recalling his time with "the Rat," a wealthy, slightly older friend who has decided not to return to school. Popular culture allusions include the Beach Boys, Miles Davis, and the Mickey Mouse Club.

Characters seem to fade in and out of the narrator's life, often with little or no apparent consequence, and many are damaged in some physical and/or emotional manner. He recalls dating one young woman who had only four fingers on one hand, for example, and another who majored in

French literature and committed suicide. In his first novel Murakami also introduces the smoky setting of J's Bar, an underground joint frequented by the narrator and the Rat. The bar is run by a wise Chinese immigrant known only as J, who lives alone with a cat with a mangled paw.

The act of writing also plays a major role in Murakami's first novel: the narrator frames the story with references to his inspiration, a fictional science fiction writer who committed suicide by jumping off the Empire State Building. In the present the Rat writes novels with no scenes of sex or death and mails them at Christmastime to the narrator. Murakami imbues the entire novel with his wry, offbeat sense of humor in which a very thin line exists between sarcasm and sincerity—a trait that characterizes most of his literary output.

Pinball, 1973

Winning the Gunzo prize compelled Murakami to write another novel about his unnamed narrator and the Rat. In 1980, he published *Pinball, 1973,* which covers the time period of 1969–1973 in the lives of the two friends. Murakami changed his narrative approach, however, and the chapters alternate between a first-person narrative and a third-person account of the Rat's failing romance and increasing depression. In later works Murakami would develop his shifting points of view in some inventive ways.

At the age of twenty-four, the narrator seems to be drifting, both professionally and emotionally, throughout *Pinball, 1973.* He is living in Tokyo and working listlessly as

In *Pinball, 1973*, Murakami started to experiment with alternating points of view.

a commercial translator. In a dreamlike twist, he awakens one day to find identical twins in bed with him. Unable to distinguish between the two girls, the narrator names them 208 and 209, after numbers on a pair of sweatshirts he gives them. They stay for months and even stage a quasi-religious burial for a broken electrical switch panel. In Murakami's fictional universe, common objects frequently take on special significance—though that significance often remains unclear.

The Quest Motif

In *Pinball, 1973,* the narrator tries to find meaning by searching for another pinball machine like the one he used to play in college. This early use of the quest motif serves as a template for many of the novels Murakami would eventually write. The narrator's nostalgic affection for the pinball machine leads to a frigid, deserted warehouse that once stored slaughtered chickens. For Murakami's narrators, the quest often brings them to other dimensions of existence. Although he finds his beloved pinball machine, the eerie experience is at best unnerving. Once he returns to his apartment and the twins, the narrator spends half an hour soaking in a hot bath to erase the smell of death that suffused the warehouse.

Throughout the novel the narrator and the Rat, now living in Kobe, never meet. As the novel progresses, the Rat eventually breaks off his romance with a woman and decides to leave town for good. In one scene J, the bartender, offers Rat some advice that resonates throughout Murakami's writings: "if a person would just make the effort, there's something to be learned from everything. From even the most ordinary, commonplace things, there's always something you can learn."

Pinball, 1973 is an even slighter novel than the first, but it too won an award: the publisher Kodansha's Shinjin Bungaku Prize for Best Newcomer in 1980. Murakami was becoming a famous name in Japan, but his next novel would propel him into international recognition.

Murakami has referred to his first two novels as "weak," and neither *Hear the Wind Sing* nor *Pinball, 1973* has ever been translated in the English-speaking world. Copies of the two novels translated into English by Alfred Birnbaum exist only in Japan. Murakami's publisher Kodansha printed those versions for use in English language classes: they have become coveted collectibles for Murakami fans all over the world.

Stories and Translations

At the same time he was working on his second novel, Murakami began to produce short stories published in Japanese magazines; he also started a successful career as a translator. Years of loving and reading literature in English prompted Murakami to translate some of his favorite American authors, including Fitzgerald, Capote, and a contemporary author who would have a profound effect on Murakami's writing, Raymond Carver. Regarding the act of translating, Murakami has said: "Translation is a kind of vehicle. One time you can write F. Scott Fitzgerald and one time Raymond Chandler. It's a transformation."

Culture Clash

Murakami has stated more than once that with his first novel, *Hear the Wind Sing,* he tried to create a new style. Part of his motivation for doing so was the extremely traditional sense of culture in Japan. In his experimental approach, he made a conscious decision to break with the style of such respected Japanese authors as Kenzaburo Oe, who won the Nobel Prize for Literature in 1994. As Murakami told *Publisher's Weekly* in 1991:

> You have to know that writing in Japan for Japanese people is in a particular style, very stiff. If you are a Japanese novelist you have to write that way. It's kind of a society, a small society, critics and writers, called high literature. . . . I want to test Japanese culture and Japanese writing from outside of Japan.

Reaction to Murakami's first novels was decidedly mixed. Many admirers of traditional Japanese literature and culture—both in Japan and abroad—were unhappy with his jazzy prose and casual references to Western popular culture. Regarding the influence of foreign writers on his work, Murakami has offered this observation: "Many Japanese critics have taken me to task for this aspect of my writing."

One critic even derided Murakami's writings as nothing more than "disposable entertainment." Yet Murakami had only just begun to establish his literary career, and his third novel would propel him into international fame.

A New Lifestyle

In 1981 Murakami and Yoko sold Peter Cat, and he began working full time on his writing career. While writing his third novel Murakami also made an abrupt change in lifestyle. He stopped smoking, began to eat healthy foods, and took up long-distance running. Since then he has run a number of competitive marathons all over the world. As Rubin points out in his book *Haruki Murakami and the Music of Words*: "This physical discipline is inseparable from the enormous professional discipline that has kept Murakami so astonishingly productive year after year."

Breakthrough and Experimentation

Murakami regards his third novel, *A Wild Sheep Chase,* which appeared in 1982, as his real debut. Although it also features the same narrator as his first two books, he develops his characters and themes into an intricate and at times wild tale of one man's search to find a sheep and a friend. Murakami may have been heavily influenced by Chandler's detective novels, but he was determined to write a different kind of mystery, one without any definite solution.

Long-distance running became a part of Murakami's life in 1981 and has remained a key element of his daily discipline. In his 2008 memoir, *What I Talk About When I Talk About Running*, he wrote about the essential linkage between his daily run and the practice of writing.

A Wild Sheep Chase

With his third novel Murakami decided to expand the tale of his unnamed narrator and the Rat, and their reluctant advance into adulthood. As the story begins, the narrator is twenty-nine years old: he is the co-owner of an advertising agency, and his wife has left him. He has not seen the Rat in a long time but suddenly receives two letters from him. One includes a photograph: a pastoral scene of a hillside in northern Japan where some sheep are grazing. Because the Rat asks him to publicize the photo in some way, the narrator uses it in an ad campaign. Meanwhile he has become involved with an unnamed ear model who moves in with him (ears feature prominently in a number of Murakami's works).

As the novel progresses the narrator is approached by a shadowy figure, a lieutenant working for a mysterious "Boss," to find one of the sheep that appears in the ad. This sheep has a strange star-shaped marking on its back. The lieutenant reveals that the animal has the power to possess people and even possessed the Boss for almost forty years. The narrator must find the sheep or the lieutenant threatens to ruin him and his business. Murakami builds on one of his major plot devices: a character has a quest thrust upon him or her and pursues it almost reluctantly.

The narrator and his nameless ear model travel to the northern island of Hokkaido, the only place where sheep exist in Japan. The narrator appears to be searching for the sheep but is actually looking for the Rat (who first sent him the photo). At one point the ear model, who seems some-

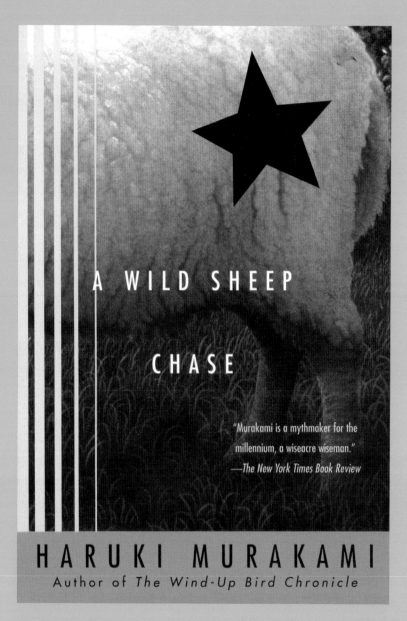

A WILD SHEEP

CHASE

"Murakami is a mythmaker for the
millennium, a wiseacre wiseman."
—*The New York Times Book Review*

HARUKI MURAKAMI
Author of *The Wind-Up Bird Chronicle*

Haruki Murakami devoted himself to writing full time in 1981.
The result: the publication of his third novel, *A Wild Sheep Chase*, to
international acclaim.

what psychic, prompts the narrator to stay at the Dolphin Hotel, where the same photo of the grazing sheep hangs on a wall. At the hotel they meet the old Sheep Professor, a retired academic who knows about the strange sheep and how to find it.

From the island of Hokkaido, the narrator and his girlfriend take a train to a mountain village far north, the scene which appears in the photo. As winter approaches, his quest ultimately leads the narrator deep into the woods, to a cabin owned by the Rat's family. The Rat is gone—and his girlfriend disappears suddenly—but the narrator takes up residence and begins to clean the house in a ritualistic fashion. At one point he meets the bizarre Sheep Man, a character who seems to step right out of a nightmare. A refugee from society and history, he is dressed in a ridiculous sheep costume and speaks in dialogue that appears with no spaces between words.

The narrator finally learns that the Rat has committed suicide, and one night his dead friend appears to him for a final conversation. Murakami cleverly blurs the line between whether this conversation actually takes place or exists solely in the narrator's mind. It is the emotion—especially the sense of loss—that becomes most important. In the final scene the narrator returns to J's Bar, but he does not tell J what has happened to the Rat. As the novel ends the narrator cries openly on the shore for the loss of his friend.

International Success

A Wild Sheep Chase garnered Murakami widespread acclaim. The *New York Times* called the novel "a bold new advance in international fiction," and *Newsday* proclaimed that the author belonged "in the topmost rank of writers of international stature." In 1992, Murakami told an audience at the University of California in Berkeley: "By writing *A Wild Sheep Chase* I was able to attain for myself the confidence that I could make it as a novelist." Murakami the author had arrived—but it was only the beginning.

Roger Shimomura's painting, *Nikkei Story*, tells the tale of three generations of Japanese life in America. It also captures some of the same themes that are found in Murakami's writing: a combination of dreamlike, almost surrealistic elements from both Japanese and American pop culture.

2

TRAVEL AND FAME

IN 1984, MURAKAMI MADE his first journey to the United States, where he visited two locations. He traveled to Princeton University in New Jersey to see the alma mater of F. Scott Fitzgerald, and he and Yoko visited an author he had long admired, Raymond Carver, in Washington State. In 1983 Murakami translated Carver's short-story collection, *Where I'm Calling From,* into Japanese, thereby introducing the American author to Japan. After Carver died from cancer in 1988, Murakami wrote: "Raymond Carver was without question the most valuable teacher I have ever had and also the greatest literary comrade."

Experimentation

In 1985 Murakami produced one of his most surreal works, the fantastical *Hard-Boiled Wonderland and the End of the World*. In this novel Murakami stepped completely into the realm of science fiction and fantasy. He split his novel into two first-person narrations, using the formal Japanese "I" (*watashi*) for the first storyline and the more intimate "I" (*boku*) for the fantasyland of the second. Because these distinctions do not exist in English, the translator, Alfred Birnbaum, decided to separate the chapters into past and present tense to delineate narrative threads.

In the odd-numbered chapters—the *Hard-Boiled Wonderland* sections—the narrative "I" is a young technician whose mind has been reprogrammed. He enters a strange underground world, beneath Tokyo, where an old scientist wants his help with decoding "the hidden language of bones." He soon becomes caught in a battle between two warring technological factions, the Calcutecs and the Semiotecs.

In the even-numbered chapters another narrator, part of the first narrator's consciousness, is a librarian who studies the dreams that exist in animal skulls in a strange and dying land. His shadow has been cut off from him and has a separate existence, a nod to Hans Christian Andersen's fairy tale, "The Shadow." Murakami won Japan's prestigious Tanizaki Prize for *Hard-Boiled Wonderland and the End of the World*. Rubin has observed that the novel "is Murakami's most elaborate exploration of the relationship of the brain to the world it perceives."

First Million-Seller

In 1986, Murakami and his wife decided to leave Japan to try living in various parts of the world. Murakami was feeling lost and wanted to get out of Japan and away from Japanese society for a while. The couple spent three years in Europe (1986–1989) and four in the United States (1991–1995). While living in Greece and Italy, Murakami composed what would be his most successful work to that date: the coming-of-age novel *Norwegian Wood*, which appeared in 1987 and became one of the best-selling novels ever published in Japan.

Norwegian Wood

After *Hard-Boiled Wonderland and the End of the World,* Murakami decided to flex his literary muscles by crafting a more straightforward story for *Norwegian Wood*. He took the title for his fifth novel from the Beatles' song of the same name. "I had never written that kind of straight, simple, rather sentimental story and I wanted to test myself," Murakami told the *Guardian* in 2003. Yet, even the linear *Norwegian Wood* is bathed in the twilight of memory: the narrator, Toru, is now thirty-seven and reflecting on the novel's events.

Toru recalls his days as a college student in 1969: he has lost a friend to suicide and has fallen in love with his dead friend's girlfriend, Naoko. He pursues Naoko to a sanatorium, where she appears to be recuperating from mental problems, but she too commits suicide. A second girlfriend, the earthy and insightful Midori, tries to help Toru move beyond the sorrow in his life. Ultimately, Toru must accept the loss of both his friend and Naoko—and he must integrate that sorrow into his everyday life.

Instant Success

With its youthful narrator and sad tale of lost love and early death, *Norwegian Wood* was an instant success for a generation of Japanese youth. The book sold more than two million hardcover copies and became Japan's *Catcher in the Rye*. (Murakami eventually translated J. D. Salinger's novel into Japanese.) Inundated with letters from admiring fans, he suddenly faced a celebrity he had never wanted. Many assumed that the story was autobiographical, but Murakami has always insisted that it is not. Instead, he took the culture of that turbulent time, 1969–1970, and used it as a setting for his melancholic novel.

Although *Norwegian Wood* was first translated into English in 1989, that version—translated by Birnbaum—was only released in Japan. Kodansha, Murakami's publisher, decided to delay publishing *Norwegian Wood* in the English-speaking world until 2000. At that time Murakami authorized a second English translation by Jay Rubin. Reviewing the novel in the *New York Times,* Janice P. Nimura commented that "although what Toru narrates never ventures into the surreal, his story proves that 'ordinary' love is no less rich and strange."

Return to Form

For his sixth novel Murakami returned to a familiar subject: the unnamed narrator of his first three novels. Following the celebrity and madness of *Norwegian Wood*'s success, he felt compelled to revisit this earlier subject matter. *Dance, Dance, Dance* appeared in Japan in 1988, although Murakami wrote it while living in Rome.

As the novel opens, the narrator searches for Kiki, the ear model who vanished in *A Wild Sheep Chase*. His quest first brings him back to the Dolphin Hotel, where he meets an attractive and elusive desk clerk named Yumiyoshi and a slightly belligerent and rather psychic teenage girl named Yuki. The bizarre Sheep Man also makes an appearance in the novel and offers some cryptic advice to the baffled narrator. His advice culminates in the simple, "Dance. As long as the music plays," a refrain that echoes throughout the novel.

Back in Tokyo, the narrator connects with a former high school classmate who has become a famous actor. He also discovers that Kiki has been murdered, and all signs point to his old classmate as the murderer. The narrator slowly begins to function as a surrogate parent for Yuki, whose wealthy parents seem, at best, distant. Through his brotherly relationship with Yuki, he starts to find some emotional center. His advice to Yuki on dealing with loss and regret seems mostly self-directed: "People die all the time. Life is a lot more fragile than we think. So you should treat others in a way that leaves no regrets. Fairly, and if possible, sincerely."

In Japan, *Dance, Dance, Dance* sold more than a half million hardcover copies during the first six months of publication. Writing in the London *Times Literary Supplement,* Alexander Harrison observed that "the novel has a relentless pace and verve which would run the world's best blockbuster out of breath."

Visiting Scholar

In 1988, Murakami's first short story, "The Kangaroo Communiqué," was published in a literary journal in the United States. Two more of his stories appeared in the *New Yorker* in 1990. That same year, his complete works began publication in Japan, and in 1991 Murakami and Yoko moved to the United States for four years. During that time, he served as a visiting scholar at Princeton University (1991–1993) and as a lecturer at the University of California–Berkeley (1993–1995).

In 1992, Murakami told author Jay McInerney, in a *New York Times* interview, that he thought he would remain in America for some time: "but while living in America, I would like to write about Japanese society from the outside. I think that is what will increasingly define my identity as a writer." When asked what "older" Japanese critics thought of his work, Murakami replied: "They don't like me."

The Elephant Vanishes, the first English language collection of Murakami's short stories, was published in 1993. A number of Murakami's most popular stories appear in the collection, including "On Seeing the 100% Perfect Girl One Beautiful April Morning," "The Second-Bakery Attack," and "The Last Lawn of the Afternoon." "On Seeing the 100% Perfect Girl" has become a favorite of film students

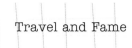

around the world: various cinematic interpretations of the story appear online.

South of the Border, West of the Sun

In his next novel, *South of the Border, West of the Sun,* which appeared in 1992, Murakami turned his attention toward the personal dilemma of a man facing a midlife crisis in his mid-thirties. Instead of focusing solely on events in the narrator's youth, Murakami addressed the emptiness and longing felt by wealthy, middle-aged professionals living in the suburbs of Tokyo.

The novel's narrator, Hajime, appears to live a perfect life: he has a lovely wife and two daughters, and he owns a pair of jazz clubs. As a boy nearing puberty, he met a lonely girl named Shimamoto who had a slight limp in her left leg. When she suddenly resurfaces as a strikingly beautiful adult woman, Hajime's seemingly stable life is thrown into an emotional tailspin. After the elusive Shimamoto warns him that there is "no middle ground" with her, he begins to question his marriage and his future. By weaving various jazz references throughout the novel, Murakami creates a somber undertone to his tale of impossible romance.

Reviewing *South of the Border, West of the Sun* in the *New York Times Book Review,* Mary Hawthorne praised the novel for "the way in which memory not only lingers but gives rise to overwhelming longing for the unreclaimable past."

Murakami Speaks

In 1992, Murakami spent four weeks at the University of California–Berkeley, where he served as Lecturer in the Humanities. In his first public speech, titled "The Sheep Man and the End of the World," he addressed the issue of being a Japanese author with an international following. Murakami discussed his resistance to the more traditional Japanese concept of "pure literature" but insisted that he was still a Japanese writer. " I want to portray Japanese society using the style that I have created," he explained. "The longer I live abroad, the stronger this desire of mine becomes."

The Wind-Up Bird Chronicle

In 1994, Murakami published his most ambitious work to date, *The Wind-Up Bird Chronicle*. The novel, which began as a short story that appeared in the *New Yorker,* involves a young man, Toru Okada, who searches for his lost cat at the same time that his wife suddenly disappears. Murakami found an inventive way to expand this story about a depressed young man who is cooking spaghetti into a complex narrative about existential and political concerns.

Cats, Wells, and Hotels

Toru's search for his cat and his wife leads him to some truly strange characters, including two psychic sisters, a rebellious teenage girl, his nefarious brother-in-law, a mother-and-son team with the preposterous names of Cinnamon and Nutmeg, and a war veteran who delivers a mysterious package from a former friend. The story is told in flashbacks, dreams, letters, and an Internet exchange. A dried-up well at a neighbor's house plays a significant role in the narrative as the aimless Toru struggles to attain some enlightenment about his unraveling life.

While at Princeton, where he wrote the novel, Murakami also researched Japan's involvement in World War II. He was particularly interested in what happened along the Mongolian and Manchurian border, and these events play a disturbing role in the novel. "I was surprised to find that it was so absurd and cruel and bloody," he told *Salon.com* in 1997. Murakami visited Manchuria and Mongolia after finishing his novel; he waited until afterward because he wanted his imagination—not history—to drive the book's events.

In *The Wind-Up Bird Chronicle,* Murakami combined many of his favorite motifs, such as cats, wells, and hotels, into a surreal detective story that reaches deep into the darkest places of the imagination. One character is a psychic prostitute, and another is a brutal killer who skins people alive. The narrator enters a parallel world by sitting at the bottom of a dark well. In his epic sweep and bizarre cast of characters, Murakami was truly flexing his imaginative muscles. Reviewing the novel in the *New York Times,* Jamie James commented that "no matter how fantastical the events it describes may be, the straight-ahead storytelling never loses its propulsive force."

In 1996, the novel won Japan's prestigious Yomiuri Literary Award. Kenzaburo Oe, the Nobel Prize–winning author who had been one of Murakami's sharpest critics, even presented the award. Writing in the *New Yorker* in 1996, Ian Buruma noted that Murakami "always wanted to apply his literary imagination to political ideas. *The Wind-Up Bird Chronicle* is his most serious attempt to do so."

Shockwaves

In 1995, Japan suffered two catastrophic events. A devastating earthquake struck the city of Kobe, Murakami's boyhood home, on January 17. More than six thousand people lost their lives, and Murakami's parents' home was destroyed. In March of that same year, Japan experienced its worst act of domestic terrorism when a religious group, Aum Shinrikyo, released poisonous sarin gas into the Tokyo subway system.

Both events had a profound effect on Murakami, who returned to Japan in 1995. "I thought 1995 was a turning point for our society," he told *Time* magazine in 2002. "At the same time, it was a turning point for me. I made up my mind that I had to commit to my society again." Deciding that too much attention had been focused on the perpetrators of the gas attack, Murakami interviewed many of the victims, along with some cult members. He also attended the trials of the cult members and published his interviews in two volumes, *Underground I & II,* appearing in 1997 and 1998.

In his introduction to the first volume, Murakami explained his goal: "I wanted, if at all possible, to get away

Haruki Murakami wrote a play called *Underground*, in response to the horrific release of poison gas in the Tokyo subway in 1995 by Japanese terrorist group Aum Shinrikyo. Actors rehearsed the play in an unfinished subway station in Berlin.

In 1995, a devastating earthquake destroyed much in the city of Kobe, Japan, including Murakami's childhood home. It was one of two terrible events that year that made him recommit to Japanese society after years abroad. It also led him to write a volume of stories called *After the Quake*. All the stories focused on a turning point in the main character's life, as had the quake in his life.

from any formula; to recognize that each person on the subway that morning had a face, a life, a family, hopes and fears, contradictions and dilemmas—and that all these factors had a place in the drama." *Kirkus Reviews* called *Underground* "a rattling chronicle of violence and terror," and in 1999 it won the prestigious Kuwabara Takeo Prize for nonfiction in Japan.

The Kobe earthquake prompted a different response from Murakami—but one also involving the story of individual lives. *After the Quake,* a collection of six short stories, appeared in 2000. Although Murakami set the stories in the time of the actual earthquake, he focused on a telling moment, a turning point, in each character's life. Main characters include a man who finds a giant frog in his apartment, another raised to believe he is the son of God, and "a born short-story writer" who loses his girlfriend to his best friend and then wins her back.

Sputnik Sweetheart

Following the success of the epic *The Wind-Up Bird Chronicle,* Murakami returned to the subject of melancholic love in *Sputnik Sweetheart,* which appeared in 1999. In this elegantly written novel, a college student simply known as K recalls his intense love for Sumire, a beautiful young woman who wants to be a writer. Their love remains platonic, however, because Sumire is in love with a wealthy older woman named Miu. While vacationing with Miu in the Greek isles, Sumire suddenly vanishes without explanation. After trying to help Miu find her, K returns to his teaching in Tokyo but remains trapped in the memory of his unfulfilled love for Sumire.

Throughout the novel, Murakami builds on the image of the dog Laika, locked into *Sputnik II* and propelled into space by the Soviets in November 1957. The three central characters seem lost within their own personalities and unable to completely enter each other's orbit. For Miu, this image is reinforced by her recollection of being trapped one night in the car of an old Ferris wheel, high above a small town in Switzerland. "Why do people have to be this lonely," K asks himself. "Was the earth put here just to nourish human loneliness?"

Reviewing the novel in *BookPage,* Bruce Tierney observed that "Murakami again displays the minimalist craftsmanship that has made him a critic's darling both in Asia and the West. Perhaps better than any contemporary writer, he captures and lays bare the raw human emotion of longing."

Murakami and the Darkness

In November 2000, Murakami gave a talk at the New School for Social Research, a college in New York City, and addressed the frequent use of darkness in his works. He told the audience: "One of the themes in my work is the dark side, of life, of society. We have our own underground— our own darkness—in ourselves, and monsters and worms living in the darkness. From time to time they come out to harm us, and we have to fight."

This Albanian postage stamp depicts Laika, the dog sent into space on *Sputnik II*.

Kafka on the Shore

In 2002, Murakami released his tenth novel, which was also his most commercially successful to that date. On the day of its publication, *Kafka on the Shore* climbed immediately to the top of the Japanese best-seller charts. Within two months, the novel had sold 460,000 copies.

In this inventive novel Murakami blends history, myth, and dreams in the epic story of two unlikely figures: a fifteen-year-old runaway named Kafka Tamura and an elderly wanderer, Satoru Nakata, who talks to cats and has a weak shadow. In a variant on the Oedipus myth, teenaged Kafka fears he is destined to commit incest with his lost mother and sister. Nakata has suffered a strange occurrence as a child, during World War II, when a flash in the sky sent him into a two-week coma and left him with no memory.

Murakami deftly relates these two stories in parallel narratives driven by each character's journey, both geographic and personal. Kafka is running away from an abusive father, whereas Nakata has taken on the task of finding a missing cat named Goma. The separate paths of both characters are peopled by a curious cast of characters, including an androgynous librarian who befriends Kafka, some cats that converse with Nakata, and a violent apparition that looks exactly like the figure of Johnnie Walker on a bottle of scotch. As the novel progresses, the tales of the two wanderers slowly converge.

The *New York Times Book Review* named *Kafka on the Shore* one of the "10 Best Books of 2005." Reviewing the novel in the *New Yorker,* John Updike called it "a real page-turner, as well as an insistently metaphysical mind-bender." Murakami had taken yet another step toward an international fame unknown by any other Japanese author.

Murakami—Storyteller

In 2005 Murakami felt a strong urge to write a series of short stories. Within a month he had finished five new ones, published that year in Japan as *Strange Tales from Tokyo.* Those stories were translated into English and gathered with nineteen others, originally published over the course of Murakami's career, into the 2006 collection, *Blind Willow, Sleeping Woman.* Murakami wrote a special introduction for the collection, which includes one of his most beloved works, the jazz-infused short story "Tony Takitani" (which was turned into a film in Japan in 2004).

After Dark

For his eleventh novel, Murakami crafted a much shorter work than many of his previous books. Set in Tokyo, *After Dark,* first appearing in 2007 (translated into English in 2007), describes one night between midnight and dawn in the intersecting lives of a few characters. Throughout the novel, Murakami employs a plural first-person point of view, drawing in readers by using "we." His descriptions reveal a cinematic approach, as angles pan in and out on various scenes. Music, hotels, sisters, and sleep surface once again as dominant motifs in the lives of the night people who populate *After Dark.*

In *After Dark*, the action takes place in the dark streets of late-night Tokyo.

On the dark side of life in Tokyo, love hotels abound.

The work of Japanese artist Aiko Nakagawa in *Love Monster Come to Me Again* pictures the subterranean night life that feels like a character in Murakami's *After Dark*.

The novel circles around Mari, a young student sitting and reading at a table in an all-night Denny's. When the jazz trombonist Takahashi interrupts her solace, Mari finds herself drawn into the seedy world of love hotels, where a Chinese immigrant prostitute has been beaten by one of her businessmen customers. Because Mari speaks some Chinese, the hotel manager, a large, burly woman named Kaoru, asks for her help. Meanwhile, Mari's sister, Eri, has been sleeping for two straight months: she lies immobile in a room where the circuits of a television are somehow tied to the sleeping beauty's consciousness and to the crime that has taken place. In this short, atmospheric novel, Murakami breathes haunting life into the white noise surrounding his twilight characters.

Writing in the *San Francisco Chronicle,* Juvenal Acosta described *After Dark* as "a bittersweet novel . . . set in half-empty diners, dark streets, and hotel rooms straight out of the paintings of Edward Hopper." Murakami won the coveted Franz Kafka Prize in 2006. The prize was named for the Czech-born novelist known for his own wildly imaginative works.

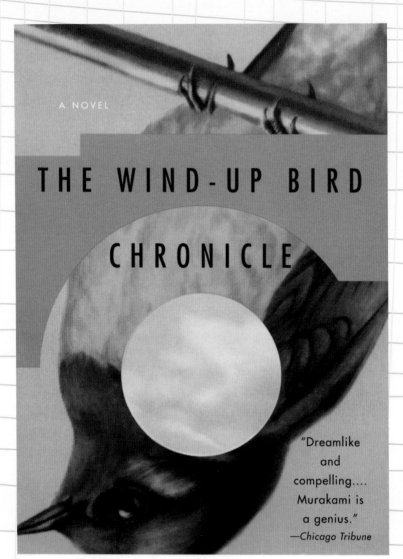

A NOVEL

THE WIND-UP BIRD

CHRONICLE

"Dreamlike
and
compelling....
Murakami is
a genius."
—Chicago Tribune

HARUKI MURAKAMI

AUTHOR OF *KAFKA ON THE SHORE*

The Wind-Up Bird Chronicle is one of Murakami's most complicated works, and one of his most wildly popular novels.

THE WIND-UP BIRD CHRONICLE

THE WIND-UP BIRD CHRONICLE, published in English in 1997, is one of Murakami's most complex works. More than six hundred pages long, it is also his longest novel to date. Although it has an epic scope, the novel features a typical Murakami narrator: a young man of thirty who finds himself at a crossroads in his life. His quest to find his wife, his cat, and some meaning in his life takes him on a psychological journey that is both detective story and historical commentary. Murakami had researched Japan's involvement in World War II before writing *The Wind-Up Bird Chronicle,* and he found some imaginative ways to work this disturbing chapter of Japan's colonial history into his kaleidoscopic novel.

Plot

Murakami separates *The Wind-Up Bird Chronicle* into three sections that were sold as separate volumes in Japan: *Book*

One: The Thieving Magpie, *Book Two: Bird as Prophet*, and *Book Three: The Birdcatcher*. Various narratives weave in and out of each book, and they take many forms, including memories, dreams, letters, computer files, and newspaper accounts.

Book One: The Thieving Magpie. June and July 1984

Toru Okada, the story's narrator, has quit his job as a "gofer" at a Tokyo law firm. He is married to Kumiko, an editor at a health foods magazine, and they live with their cat in a quiet suburb. A strange phone call interrupts Toru one morning as he is cooking spaghetti and listening to an opera, Gioachino Rossini's *The Thieving Magpie*. An unknown woman on the other end seems to know everything about his life, but she hangs up abruptly.

Kumiko then calls and tells Toru that their cat is missing and that he needs to search the neighborhood for him. Their cat shares its name with Kumiko's brother, a shadowy politician named Noboru Wataya. From his kitchen window, Toru hears the "mechanical cry of a bird that sounded as if it were winding a spring." Kumiko had given it the name "the wind-up bird." This sound echoes throughout the novel.

As Toru searches the neighborhood for his cat, he enters a narrow alley that "had neither entrance nor exit." The alley leads to an empty house: in the garden stands a stone statue of a bird with its wings spread, ready for flight but frozen in time. There, Toru meets May Kasahara, a sixteen-year-old dropout with a flippant attitude. The two become instant friends, and, like a number of Murakami's teenage characters, she often functions as a voice of reason for Toru. She also refers to Toru as "Mr. Wind-Up Bird."

The next day Kumiko calls from work and asks Toru to meet a woman named Malta Kano at a restaurant for help with finding the cat. Malta turns out to be clairvoyant and has a sister named Creta, who also has psychic abilities and who claims she was raped by Kumiko's brother, Noboru Wataya. Malta warns Toru that he is entering a new phase in his life.

Toru then relates the story of meeting Kumiko and her family, especially his first encounter with her belligerent brother, Noboru. He also recalls their visits to old Mr. Honda, a psychic, spiritual advisor, and friend of Kumiko's family. Malta's sister Creta comes to visit Toru and tells him the story of her difficult life, which has included a suicide attempt and work as a prostitute. It was in this capacity that she met Noboru Wataya.

Toru receives a visit from the war veteran Lieutenant Mamiya, an old army friend of Mr. Honda. He has a prosthetic left hand and is delivering a package from Mr. Honda, who has died. Mamiya tells the story of his service with the Japanese army in Manchuria during World War II, when he and his friend Yamamoto were captured and tortured by the Mongolians. He watched as his friend was skinned alive by a brutal Russian named Boris the Manskinner.

Mamiya then describes how he was left to die in the bottom of a well, where he had a revelation in the timeless darkness but could not understand it. Mr. Honda had predicted that Mamiya would not die on the Asian continent, and he survived. After Mamiya leaves, Toru discovers that the box from Mr. Honda is empty.

Book Two: Bird as Prophet.
July to October 1984

As *Book Two* opens, Kumiko does not return home from work. Creta Kano then appears to Toru in a vivid dream and has psychic sex with him. He realizes his search for his wife means he must also search his consciousness for the truth. Toru meets Malta and Noboru at a tearoom, where his brother-in-law informs him that Kumiko has left him for another man. Toru, who stands up to Noboru during the conversation, warns his politically powerful brother-in-law that he is willing to strike back.

Distraught over the loss of his wife, Toru finds an old, dry well in his neighborhood and decides to hide there for days, trying to reach another state of consciousness. His time spent in the dark well leads Toru's mind to a strange otherworldly hotel and to the dangerous Room 208, where he encounters a number of the novel's women and a shadowy figure wielding a knife. He spends most of his time in the darkness pondering his marriage to Kumiko. At one point Toru emerges from the well with a strange, dark-blue mark on his cheek.

While watching people at a train station in Shinjuku, Toru suddenly recognizes a folksinger carrying a guitar. Toru and Kumiko had listened to this folksinger three years earlier, when Kumiko had a secret abortion. Toru now

The bird has symbolic powers in Murakami's novel, *The Wind-Up Bird Chronicle.*

views this night and the loss of their child as the point where his relationship with his wife began to unravel. He follows the musician to an apartment building; the man attacks Toru with a baseball bat, but Toru wrests it from him and violently beats him. Afterward, he becomes more convinced than ever that he must find Kumiko.

Book Three: The Birdcatcher.
October 1984 to December 1985

Toru decides to buy the land with the abandoned house and dried-out well in his neighborhood. Back at Shinjuku train station, he meets Nutmeg Akasaka, a beautiful businesswoman who runs a healing clinic for empty women. Recognizing the special properties of the mark on Toru's cheek—her father bore the same mark—Nutmeg employs Toru as a healer and agrees to help him purchase the house he wants to buy.

Meanwhile, May has left Toru's neighborhood and is staying somewhere in the mountains and working at a wig factory. She writes letters to Toru; they appear throughout *Book Three*, but he never receives them. This section also includes newspaper accounts of strange happenings at the mysterious house Toru has purchased with Nutmeg and her silent son Cinnamon (they are using it as a base of operations). The negative newspaper stories begin to affect Noboru's political standing.

Toru finally finds his cat, now missing for a year, and renames him Mackerel. He also returns to the well, where he once again "sees" the strange hotel suite: Room 208. Still, he cannot yet pass through the wall of the well to enter the room.

Nutmeg tells Toru the story of her father, a veterinarian sent by Japan to work in a zoo in Manchuria during World War II. As a boy he also heard the call of the wind-up bird, and his cheek bore the same magical mark that appears on Toru's face. Along with his family, including Nutmeg as a child, the veterinarian witnesses a terrible attack by Japanese soldiers who are ordered to kill all the animals in the zoo. He is also present at the brutal beating with a baseball bat of Chinese prisoners. Nutmeg explains that she related these stories to Cinnamon when he was a child, but he suddenly stopped talking.

Toru then receives a visit from a strange little man who is named Ushikawa who works for Noboru. Ushikawa claims that Noboru will help Toru reconcile with Kumiko only if he will abandon his involvement with the mysterious house, which has created negative publicity for Noboru's political career. Toru angrily refuses to make a deal with Ushikawa, however, setting up battle lines with his powerful brother-in-law.

Nutmeg and Cinnamon then take up residence in the house in Toru's neighborhood. Meanwhile, the press keeps hounding Noboru about his family's involvement in the house. Toru discovers secret documents Cinnamon has filed on a computer in the house: the documents are named "The Wind-Up Bird Chronicles." Through the computer, Toru receives e-mail from Kumiko, who tells him to forget her. At the same time Toru receives a letter from Lieutenant

Mamiya describing his reunion with Boris the Manskinner in a concentration camp in Siberia, Russia.

Back down the well, Toru finally achieves a state of consciousness in which he can pass through the wall and enter the strange hotel room. He follows a waiter, whistling Rossini's *The Thieving Magpie,* into Room 208. Once in the room, Toru sees Noboru's face on a television screen: a news report claims that someone has hit the politician with a baseball bat. He also meets a strange woman who at times sounds exactly like Kumiko. He tells her he wants to bring her home, but she is resistant. Instead, she gives him "a present," a baseball bat. A shadowy figure—a man—then appears and tries to attack Toru with a knife, but he smashes him with the baseball bat in the darkness.

Toru returns to reality in the well, only to find that it is filling up with water. He recalls a prophetic warning from Mr. Honda: "Be careful of water." Saved at the last minute by Cinnamon, he awakens to find Nutmeg and Cinnamon watching over him. Nutmeg informs Toru that, in reality, Noboru passed out at a dinner following a press conference. On the computer, Toru opens up one of the wind-up chronicles and finds a letter from Kumiko. In it, she tells Toru that she can never reunite with him and that she has decided she must kill her brother.

In the final scene Toru visits May, and she discovers that he has never received her letters. He informs her that Kumiko is in jail for killing her brother but that he intends to wait for her. They say good-bye, and a low winter moon follows Toru as he takes the train back to his home.

Themes and Issues

The Wind-Up Bird Chronicle is a mysterious, dreamlike novel that still manages to address both personal and political concerns relevant to the modern reader. Its themes are far-reaching—from the difficulty of knowing oneself to the pressures of social conformity. Murakami masterfully blends the novel's many themes into a captivating narrative about one man's search for his wife.

Murakami has described the special world he creates in his imaginative novels: "When I write fiction, especially long novels, I am able to go to a different world. That world is *totally* different from this actual, present world. I live in that new world and write daily reports from there. How can we move to that world? The rule is simple: you should go through the stone walls that surround you. How can we go through the stone walls? I don't know. I have no exact idea. But that happens to me when the time is right, and I am ready to go. I call it Puff, the Magic Dragon."

The Difficult Search for Self-Identity

Toru's quest to find his wife and his cat leads to a more personal search for self-awareness. Whereas many of Murakami's earlier narrators seem somewhat cool and detached, especially about personal losses in their lives, Toru is determined to bring meaning back into his life. In 2002, Murakami told *Time* magazine: "Now, what my protagonists seek is peace of mind."

For Toru, this challenge is a difficult one: as the novel opens, he has no work and seems uninterested in his future. Only by entering a higher state of existence can Toru achieve any enlightenment about himself. The psychic Creta, who also spends time down the well, tells Toru after she joins him in his consciousness: "Without a true self . . . a person can not go on living. It is like the ground we stand on." To discover who he really is, Toru must face the truth about his marriage, and he must find the strength to stand up to his powerful brother-in-law. As he observes at the end of *Book Two*, he has to find Kumiko to find himself: "With my own hands, I had to pull her back into *this world*. Because if I didn't, that would be the end of me. This person, this self that I thought of as 'me,' would be lost."

Different Planes of Existence

As in most of Murakami's fiction, many planes of existence surface throughout the novel. Reality does not simply consist of the here and now. Toru and Lt. Mamiya share the mind-expanding experience of staying down a well for a number of days. The darkness and sensory deprivation lead both men to a heightened awareness of reality. In Toru's case, the experience also leads to entering another mental state, represented by the eerie Room 208. In that mental space, Kumiko, Creta, and the strange woman on the phone seem to merge into one being. When he finally reaches Room 208, Toru appears to reconnect with Kumiko, merging with her subconscious representative as he beats Noboru. As in a fairy tale, she gives him an object, a baseball bat, which helps him to defeat his enemy, Noboru. Also, many of the characters in the novel are psychic, including Mr. Honda, Malta, and Creta. Creta describes herself as a "prostitute of the mind" and can enjoy sex in a dream state. Murakami told *Salon. com* in 1997: "The subconscious is very important to me as a writer."

The Burden of History

One of the main subplots of the novel involves Japan's colonial actions in Manchuria during World War II. When Lt. Mamiya arrives at Toru's doorstep, he brings with him stories of the bloody fighting, especially in the "forgotten" Battle of Nomonhan in 1939. Thousands died in this undeclared border war between Japan and the Soviet Union.

As Matthew Strecher points out in his book on *The Wind-Up Bird Chronicle*: "Mamiya's narrative is a horrifying one . . . and represents a new level of graphic violence in Murakami fiction." Murakami connects the events of World War II with Toru's predicament by relating them to Noboru's background: Noboru's uncle, Yoshitaka Wataya, was involved in Japan's failed and costly war against China. Noboru and his faceless authority represent the power of the state—the same state that waged the Battle of Nomonhan. On this level, Toru fights the same shadowy enemy of individualism that forced soldiers like Lt. Mamiya to take part in World War II. As Rubin observes: "*The Wind-Up Bird Chronicle* continues a debate that still rages in Japan today about the official recognition of the crimes Japan committed against the other peoples of Asia." For Murakami, facing

Here, two prisoners are held captive, victims of the war between China and Japan during the Japanese invasion of Manchuria in 1931.

these historical demons means facing the darkness that exists within all of us.

The Power of Sex

Sexual energy pervades *The Wind-Up Bird Chronicle*. As the novel opens, a mysterious woman calls Toru and tries to initiate phone sex with him. In time, Toru learns that Kumiko felt unfulfilled sexually with him and found pleasure in another man's arms. Her departure is, partially, a quest for sexual satisfaction. During one of his sexual unions with Creta, she wears Kumiko's dress, connecting her with Toru's missing wife. After one of Toru's psychic sexual encounters, he suddenly discovers the mark on his cheek—a mark that grants him special healing powers. Yet, as women rub this mark to obtain its healing force, Toru becomes aroused, emphasizing the connection between sexuality and regeneration. Strecher sees a "flow between the conscious and unconscious" in these sexual encounters.

Negative aspects of sex also surface in the novel: Creta explains that once Noboru raped her, she lost her identity and felt like "an empty container." Toru also recognizes certain sexual boundaries in his relationships with women: although he has the opportunity to take advantage of his young friend May, he never does so.

Pain

Pain plays an integral role in many of the narratives that appear throughout the novel. For most of the characters, surviving painful situations helps them to grow and to learn more about themselves. In Toru's case, he is attracted to the difficulty of remaining in the darkness of the well because he feels he must overcome his fear of it. Slowly he rises above the physical discomfort of being in one position for a long time and is therefore able to reach other states of consciousness through his pain. Lt. Mamiya relates having lost all sense of pain while he was down the well in the war: "My body felt as if it had lost all sensation." Although his leg is broken, he does not feel it until his perceptions return: "And along with the recovery of my perceptions, naturally enough, came the sensation of pain."

Creta describes her personal pain in purely physical terms: "All my life I have experienced physical pain with far greater frequency and intensity than others." She even attempts suicide but survives. Afterward, she can feel no pain—until she is raped by Noboru Wataya. She then begins to feel pain again but discovers a new way to deal with it: "When pain comes to me, I leave my physical self . . . so the yoke of the pain is not able to capture me," she tells Toru.

Analysis

Many of the characters in *The Wind-Up Bird Chronicle* seem almost like emanations of Toru's mind. They often appear as if out of nowhere, and many simply vanish without a trace from the story line. Some exist solely within Toru's dreams, whereas others seem to merge into different characters. Ultimately, Toru must integrate all these characters—the good and the evil—to reach his ultimate goal of knowing himself.

Characters

Toru Okada

At first glance, Toru may seem like a typical Murakami protagonist. He is thirty, out of work, lacks ambition, and has no interest in making large sums of money. Yet, it is Toru's voice that narrates most of the story, and it is through his eyes that we view the other characters and the events surrounding them. Early in the novel, Toru explains that he enjoys his current life of reading, food shopping, and cooking. He has become complacent, but his world is shaken when he suddenly realizes that he does not fully know his wife. Her departure serves as the catalyst for Toru to wake up and to realize that his life is not as it seems. In this sense he represents Murakami's "Everyman," a character going along with his life without realizing that he is in danger of losing everything. As Toru searches for his wife and some meaning in his life, he becomes more active. We sense his determination to overcome his controlling brother-in-law, Noboru, and his goodness in dealing with the novel's many women characters. From May to Creta to Nutmeg, Toru behaves in an understanding and compassionate manner. Yet, this trait also returns us to the original question: How, then, can he know so little about his own wife?

Kumiko

Kumiko, Toru's wife, is an elusive character in the novel. On the surface she appears to be a happily married young professional. We meet her briefly, early in the book, when she returns home and seems distant and aggravated. After her disappearance, her life comes out slowly, and we learn—through letters and e-mails—that she has been unfaithful to Toru, has had an abortion and did not tell him, and was abused by her brother Noboru. Therefore, Kumiko has been hiding her other self, a dissatisfied woman with a secret life. Like Toru, Kumiko takes action by the end of the novel. On the subconscious level, she gives Toru the bat that enables him to beat Noboru in Room 208. On the conscious level, as she explains in her final e-mail to Toru, she has been holding on to the hope that he would free her from the pain of her brother's defilement. When she pulls the plug on her brother's life support system, she also frees herself from her past and accepts her punishment.

May Kasahara

Sixteen-year-old May Kasahara comes from a long line of Murakami teenage girls who speak with insight and wisdom far beyond their years. In this sense she most closely resembles Yuki in *Dance, Dance, Dance*. May's family is nonexistent throughout the novel. She has dropped out of school yet seems to live on her own, working part-time for a wig company. She tells Toru: "I hate history"—and in her own way she exists outside the novel's other events. May becomes a touchstone for Toru, a person to whom he can turn when he needs to discuss his feelings and his fears. She is blunt with him and forces him to face many difficult questions, such as: would he ever take his wife back knowing she has been unfaithful? Her appearance in the final scene indicates her importance to Toru's quest for the truth.

Noboru Wataya

Kumiko's older brother, Noboru Wataya, functions as Toru's archenemy throughout the novel. He first appears in a flashback in which Toru recalls his dismissive response to the news that Toru wants to marry his sister. As the novel progresses, Noboru becomes a powerful political force. In Toru's eyes, he has great media presence but no substance. Noboru becomes one of the main obstacles hindering Toru's attempt to reunite with Kumiko. He appears to be controlling Kumiko in some way, especially when he sends his henchman, Ushikawa, to pressure Toru. Noboru also plays an important role in Creta Kano's background, for he raped her while she was working as a prostitute, leaving her with a split personality and psychic abilities. It is Creta who tells Toru that Noboru is his "exact opposite." Finally, Noboru merges with the negative man wielding a knife when Toru visits Room 208. With a little help from Kumiko, both in the physical and the subconscious worlds, Toru finally overcomes Noboru's manipulative evil.

Lt. Mamiya

Lieutenant Mamiya is a World War II veteran and a good friend of the late Mr. Honda, who served with Mamiya and was a spiritual advisor to Kumiko's family. Mamiya introduces the narrative concerning Japan's colonial involvement in Mongolia during the war. Captured by the Mongolians and thrown down a well to die, Mamiya nevertheless survives (as Mr. Honda predicted he would). Following the war, he also survives a stint in a Siberian concentration camp, although he does also lose his left hand. Still, Mamiya tells Toru that he has lived the rest of his life as an "empty shell," echoing Creta Kano's description of herself. His story becomes especially important to Toru, who is influenced by the veteran's experiences while down the well. Thematically, Mamiya brings Japan's more questionable past into the overall narrative.

Malta and Creta Kano

The Kano sisters represent important female forces in Toru's life. Kumiko first contacted Malta, a psychic, to help Toru find their cat, but Malta also connects Toru to Noboru at the tearoom. Through Malta, Toru meets Creta, the third character who spends time down a well. Creta, who describes herself as a prostitute of the mind, bears a certain resemblance to Kumiko, merging the two women in Toru's mind. Toru has both physical and psychic sex with Creta in the course of the novel. Although she wants Toru to run away to the island of Crete with her, he refuses. Her involvement with Noboru and her warnings about him also connect Creta to Toru and reinforce Noboru's negative power.

Nutmeg and Cinnamon

The mother-and-son team of Nutmeg and Cinnamon Akasaka seem like visitors from another world. They, too, play a pivotal role in Toru's quest. Toru first meets Nutmeg, who runs a healing clinic for women, while he is sitting on a bench at a train station. She recognizes the strange mark on his cheek because her father, a veterinarian in the war, also bore that mark. The song of the wind-up bird appears in the stories she tells Toru. Nutmeg serves as a kind of patron to Toru: she puts up the money so that he can buy the abandoned house with the well in his neighborhood. Cinnamon, her silent son who communicates mostly through hand movements, also serves a helpful role in the novel: he appears when he is most needed and even comes to Toru's aid just as he is about to drown in the well. Cinnamon and Nutmeg use the house as base of operations for their healing business; from there, Cinnamon maintains strange computer files that enable Toru to reconnect with Kumiko through e-mail. Toru observes: "The depths of this computer were the very depths of Cinnamon himself."

Motifs and Symbols

Murakami employs a number of recurring motifs and symbols that help to connect the novel's various themes and narratives.

The Wind-Up Bird

The image of the wind-up bird first appears when Toru recalls that Kumiko gave that name to the "mechanical cry of a bird that sounded as if it were winding a spring." Later, May asks Toru to think up a nickname for himself. He responds, "Wind-Up Bird," and adds that the bird "winds the world's spring." The cry of the strange wind-up bird appears throughout the novel, often at critical moments. Matthew Strecher sees the bird as "a metaphor for time and history," and feels the bird exists to "set the flow of time going again."

The sound of the wind-up bird also surfaces in the stories about Nutmeg's father, the veterinarian, in World War II. In addition, Cinnamon names his computer files "The Wind-Up Bird Chronicles." Toru views the connection between his own nickname and the image's appearance in Nutmeg's stories and Cinnamon's files as a "chance conjunction." He also speculates about the bird's involvement in the events of people's lives: "Nearly all within the range of the wind-up bird's cry were ruined, lost." In this reading, the cry of the wind-up bird is stronger than the "will of human beings."

The Well

The dry, darkened well where Toru spends so much time in the novel also provides him with the opportunity to make sense out of his life. At one point Toru recalls the prophetic words of Mr. Honda: "When you're supposed to go down, find the deepest well and go down to the bottom." This motif of descent into another world recalls the ancient Greek myth of Orpheus, who goes down to the underworld to try to retrieve his wife, but, at the fateful moment, looks back and loses her forever.

The well sits on the property of an abandoned house in Toru's neighborhood—a house that has a mysterious history. Toru comments that the well's darkness has a "strange sense of significance." That darkness reflects the darkened state of Toru's mind, but it also serves as an entry into another world, a subconscious world. To enter this world, Toru must become one with the darkness in the well; he must surrender to it. "How can we move to that world," Murakami has explained. "The rule is simple: you should go through the stone walls that surround you." Once Toru enters the other world, he begins to see images: Noboru's face on a television screen, a corridor, a hotel room, a strange woman in bed, and a waiter. When Toru finally enters Room 208, he does so through the walls of the well. Upon his return, after finding Kumiko and defeating Noboru in Room 208, water reenters the well, representing the return of Toru's own life force.

The Strange Mark
The strange blue-black mark on Toru's cheek first appears after one of his visits to the well. In the darkness Toru had dreamed of passing through a wall as the telephone woman led him by the hand. He then felt a strange sensation of heat on his cheek. "Located just beyond the right cheekbone, it was about the size of an infant's palm." This description connects the mark to the abortion Kumiko had and hid from Toru. Strecher claims that the mark is "a new, embryonic consciousness, one that will live and grow in his cheek until he completes his quest. The mark also grants Toru healing abilities.

When Nutmeg sees Toru sitting on the bench, she recognizes the mark: her veterinarian father bore the same marking on his face. In Cinnamon's chronicle about his grandfather, the mark becomes a symbol of destiny. As a child the veterinarian hated the mark, but as he matured, he gradually came to accept it. "And this may have been a factor that helped form his attitude of resignation in all matters having to do with fate." The mark grants Toru special powers—but it also helps him to accept his destiny.

Room 208

Hotels play a recurring role in Murakami's writings, and they often function as portals to other planes of existence. This motif first surfaced in *The Wild Sheep Chase* and was developed further in *Dance, Dance, Dance.* Characters often find secret hallways and hidden rooms, locales that lead them to some truth. The surreal Room 208 in *The Wind-Up Bird Chronicle* exists in the subconscious "other" world Toru enters through the walls of the well. The hotel consists of a labyrinth of darkened corridors, ultimately leading to Room 208. The number of the room recalls one of the twins, 208 and 209, from *Pinball, 1973.* The woman Toru sees in Room 208 represents a combination of Kumiko, Creta, and the strange telephone woman who calls early in the novel. In this sense, the hotel room is a markedly sexual space.

Yet, the room also houses danger for Toru: it is here he first sees the shadowy figure wielding a knife. A sexual experience with the strange woman in the room leads to the emergence of the mark on Toru's cheek. Ultimately, the room is also the scene of Toru's final battle with the shadowy "Noboru" of the other world. With the help of the room's Kumiko figure, Toru finally overcomes the evil force represented by his powerful brother-in-law.

Literary Reception of the Novel

Upon the novel's English-language release in 1997, critics hailed *The Wind-Up Bird Chronicle* as a new milestone in Murakami's career. More than six hundred pages long, the novel was undeniably ambitious. Murakami's previous novels had a small audience in the rest of the world, but *The Wind-Up Bird Chronicle* established his international reputation as a major world author.

Writing in the *New York Times*, Jamie James commented that the novel "marks a significant advance in Murakami's art." Still, James felt the novel had an "uneven design" and that the war narratives seemed superimposed on the basic story line. Michiko Kakutani also reviewed the novel, in this case for the daily *New York Times*. She contended that it lacked "closure" and was "fragmentary and chaotic." Writing for *Salon.com*, Laura Miller observed that the novel "has the easy authority of the work of a natural born story-teller, and each eccentric character and odd development only adds to the anticipation that Murakami will tie it all up in a satisfying resolution."

Reviewing the novel in *Time* magazine, Pico Iyer praised the book's "series of hauntingly imagined passages" but criticized Murakami's change in tone from his earlier works: "a world of intense jazz has given over to one of easy listening." Kevin Hunsanger, in the *San Francisco Bay Guardian*, noted that "Murakami pulls the reader deeper into a world where everything is connected but nothing ever fits flush." However, Julian Ferraro, writing in the *Times Literary Supplement*, praised the novel: "The most impressive thing about Murakami's writing is his sustained delineation of a surreal, super-real world."

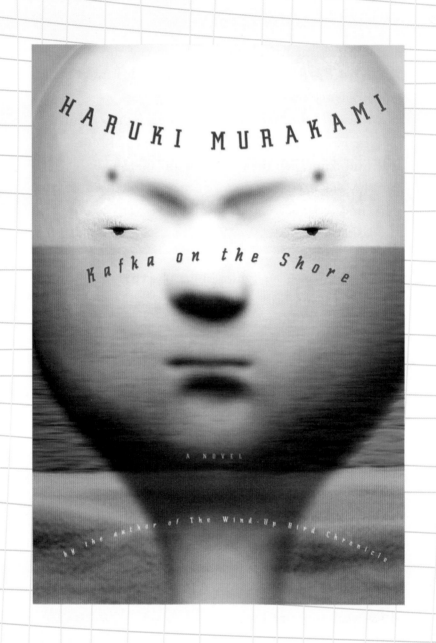

Kafka on the Shore is one of Murakami's most popular and critically esteemed novels.

4

KAFKA ON THE SHORE

KAFKA ON THE SHORE, released in English in 2005, is one of Murakami's most beloved books. After its publication in Japan, in 2002, the novel spawned a website devoted to fans asking questions about its characters and intricacies. More than 8,800 messages appeared on the site, and Murakami personally answered some 1,200 of them. The novel's wide appeal stems greatly from its fantastical story line and from its two empathetic protagonists: a fifteen-year-old runaway and a mentally challenged older man who can converse with cats.

Plot
Narrative One—Kafka's Tale

Kafka on the Shore consists of two parallel narratives. In the first, told in the novel's odd-numbered chapters, Kafka Tamura leaves his Tokyo home on the eve of his fifteenth birthday. He is running away from his abusive father,

Koichi Tamura, a famous sculptor. Kafka's mother left home when he was only four, and she took his adopted sister with her. He has never seen them, and his father has erased all memories of his mother from the boy's existence. Koichi has told Kafka that—like Oedipus in the Greek myth—the boy would one day murder his own father and sleep with his mother.

Another character simply named Crow accompanies Kafka on his journey: Crow functions as an alter ego within Kafka. Kafka also carries a photograph of himself and his sister playing on the shore. For no apparent reason, Kafka chooses the island of Shikoku as his destination. When he arrives at the station there, he meets Sakura, a young woman who tells him he can stay at her apartment for a few nights.

Kafka, who has loved libraries since he was a boy, also visits a local library. There he meets the androgynous librarian, Oshima, who is also a hemophiliac. Kafka assumes Oshima is a young man, but in time learns he is biologically a woman but lives as a man. "My body is physically female," Oshima explains, "but my mind's completely male." Kafka also meets Miss Saeki, the beautiful musician and librarian, and wonders if she could possibly be his mother.

While Oshima convinces Miss Saeki to let Kafka live in the library as his assistant, he drives the runaway to his family's mountain retreat in Kochi. Oshima reveals that Miss Saeki once had a lover, a childhood sweetheart who was also named Kafka. She wrote a popular and successful folk song called "Kafka on the Shore" for him; he was beaten to death during a student uprising when he was only twenty. An oil painting of a young man by the sea bears the same title.

At one point in the novel, Kafka awakens by a religious shrine to find he is covered with someone else's blood. Having been unconscious for hours, he has no idea how he got there or whose blood it is. Shortly thereafter, he discovers in a newspaper account that his father has been brutally murdered. Because Kafka is in Shikoku when the murder occurs, he could not—physically—have committed the crime. The following day two thousand sardines and mackerel suddenly fall from the sky near where Kafka's father was murdered. Kafka tells Oshima: "My father polluted everything he touched, damaged everyone around him."

While working at the library, Kafka slowly becomes closer to Miss Saeki, who tells him the story of her former lover named Kafka. At night she appears as a fifteen-year-old version of herself to Kafka, and he falls in love with the apparition. Eventually, he sleeps with Miss Saeki, both subconsciously and in reality. Haunted by his father's curse, Kafka cannot help wondering if Miss Saeki is also his mother.

Discovering the police are searching for him, Kafka retreats to Oshima's mountain cabin. Exploring the forests near the cabin, Kafka enters another dimension, a world where soldiers from the Japanese Imperial Army appear to be trapped in another time zone.

At a cabin deep in these woods—where "Time isn't a factor"—Kafka once again meets the figure of Miss Saeki as a fifteen-year-old. She tells him she wants him to have the painting, *Kafka on the Shore*. As he leaves this fairy-tale environment, the two soldiers warn Kafka never to look back and advise him to struggle to tell right from wrong, no matter how difficult.

When Kafka returns to the library, Oshima informs him that Miss Saeki has had a heart attack and died. Kafka decides to go back to Tokyo and to tell the police what he knows. Oshima tells him: "The world is a metaphor, Kafka Tamura." Saying good-bye to Sakura and bearing Miss Saeki's painting, Kafka takes the train back to Tokyo. In his final dialogue with Kafka, the boy named Crow offers some advice: "Look at the painting," he says. "And listen to the wind"—reminding the reader of the title of Murakami's first novel.

Narrative Two—Nakata's Tale

The second narrative of *Kafka on the Shore* is told in the third person and involves the story of Satoru Nakata. As a small boy during World War II, Nakata accompanied a group of children and their teacher on a field trip to pick mushrooms. At one point the children suddenly lapse into an unexplained coma: all of them slowly regain consciousness, except for Nakata, who remains in a coma for a few weeks. In chapters involving U. S. Army Intelligence reports, investigators determine that no poison gas or any other weapon was used in that area. However, their teacher, who was unaffected by the mass coma, eventually reveals that she had slapped Nakata repeatedly shortly before he and the other children lost consciousness.

When Nakata finally awakens, he has lost all memory of himself, his family, and the world. Although many of his higher intelligence faculties are gone, Nakata does gain the ability to converse with cats. He also refers to himself in third person, as "Nakata," and speaks in a quaint, slightly stilted manner. He also has a weakened shadow, half its normal darkness.

In the present time of the narrative, Nakata is in his sixties and works as a locater of lost cats. His search to find one cat, Goma, initiates his journey. Other cats inform Nakata that a tall man wearing a high hat and boots has stolen Goma. A large, military dog leads him to the home of Johnnie Walker, the figure from the Scotch bottle. Walker is stealing cats, killing them, storing their heads in a freezer, and eating their hearts. The dog wants Nakata to kill him: in one of Murakami's most violent scenes, the iconic advertising figure murders cats in front of the appalled Nakata, who finally and reluctantly grabs a steak knife and stabs Walker to death. Nakata passes out and then awakens in a clump of weeds; he has saved Goma, but he can no longer communicate with cats.

The following day thousands of sardines and mackerel inexplicably rain down from the sky. The police also find the murdered body of a famous sculptor stabbed to death with a steak knife by an intruder.

The rest of Nakata's narrative reads like a road trip film: he accepts rides from various truck drivers as he moves away from Tokyo. While he witnesses men beating someone at a rest area in Fujigawa, leeches suddenly pour down from the sky. Nakata then hitches a ride with Hoshino, a young truck driver in his mid-twenties, wearing a Hawaiian shirt and oversized Nikes. The two become instant friends. Nakata knows only that he wants to cross a bridge, and Hoshino agrees to take him to Shikoku (where Kafka is hiding out).

Nakata also searches for a strange "entrance stone" that leads to another world. While walking at night in the streets of Takamatsu, Hoshino meets Colonel Sanders, a Chekhov-quoting pimp dressed as the Kentucky Fried Chicken icon. Colonel Sanders explains: "I'm kind of an overseer, supervising something to make sure it fulfills its original role." This eerie character leads Hoshino to the entrance stone, hidden in a Shinto shrine, and Hoshino then brings it to Nakata. During a lightning storm, Nakata opens the entrance stone, which leads to another world.

In Shikoku, Nakata's path leads him straight to the library and to Miss Saeki, who says she has been waiting for him. Taking his hands, she acts as a conduit through which Nakata can feel "what memories are." Nakata confesses to her that he has taken the place of a fifteen-year-old boy and "murdered someone." Yet, he assures Miss Saeki he is there to "restore what's here now to the way it *should* be." She asks him to destroy three files containing a record of her life, and he agrees. Miss Saeki then dies in her office.

After Nakata and Hoshino burn Miss Saeki's files, Nakata also dies. Hoshino discovers that he, too, can now converse with cats, and one of them, named Toro, informs him that he must destroy the entrance stone. In a bloody battle with a strange white creature that crawls out of Nakata's corpse, Hoshino finally destroys the stone.

Themes and Issues

In many ways, *Kafka on the Shore* is Murakami's most demanding novel. Its dreamlike narrative often requires readers to suspend their disbelief and to accept the story's bizarre characters and fantastical occurrences. Still, the novel touches on many themes and issues familiar to readers of Murakami's fiction.

Self-Acceptance and Identity

Kafka's main quest throughout the novel not only involves running away from home—it also involves his discovery of his own identity. Once he reaches Shikoku, Kafka faces a number of decisions that help to define him. For example, because he does not judge or reject Oshima for being a biological woman who dresses like a man, Kafka receives Oshima's help and kindness. "Whatever you are, I like you," he tells Oshima. By accepting others, Kafka slowly learns to accept himself.

Kafka must also accept the limitations of his age. He says he hates being fifteen because he feels "hopeless," and he compares himself to Miss Saeki, who he says has "overcome all kinds of obstacles." These thoughts leave Kafka feeling "clueless." At times, Kafka feels as if he is "being pushed along by reality" or "shoved from behind by some huge heartbeat." However, Miss Saeki tells him he is "stronger and more independent" than she is.

Ultimately, to know himself, Kafka must accept the fact that his mother left him when he was four. As the boy named Crow tells him, Kafka must forgive her and try to understand her anguish. And Kafka must learn to believe in himself. "You did the right thing," the boy named Crow tells him as the novel ends. "You did what was best."

The Inevitability of Fate

An overwhelming sense of fate, or destiny, drives many of the novel's events. Although they never meet, the two main characters are drawn by a force that leads them to the same place. When Kafka leaves home, he has no idea where he should go, yet he somehow chooses Takamatsu on the island of Shikoku. As he observes: "Fate seems to be taking me in some stranger directions." He stumbles upon a library run by a woman who not only knew another young man named Kafka but who also wrote a song named "Kafka on the Shore"—and who owns a painting with the same title.

Oshima discusses this theme directly with Kafka. Kafka admits that he feels that he is "following a path somebody else has mapped out" for him. "Man doesn't choose fate," responds Oshima, who adds, "Fate chooses man." Oshima sees connections to "irony" and "metaphor" in the power of fate.

Nakata also embraces his fate. Although he tells Hoshino that he has no idea where he needs to go, he adds: "But I think I'll know when I get there." When Nakata meets Miss Saeki in Takamatsu, she tells him she has been expecting him: their paths seem fated to cross. In his simplicity, Nakata truly accepts his fate, even though it ultimately costs him his life.

The Strange Force of Nature

Nature plays a major role throughout *Kafka on the Shore*. As the novel opens, Nakata (as a boy) falls into a coma during a nature outing to pick mushrooms. Nature also provides the setting for a number of the novel's most significant events. After Kafka passes out and then wakes up to discover he is covered with blood, he finds himself in "a thick brush," where he smells "plants" and "dirt." While Kafka stays at Oshima's cabin in the mountains, he feels compelled to explore the nearby forests: "I want to see— and *feel*—what kind of danger lies ahead. . . . Something's shoving me forward." As he tramps forward, he discards everything he is carrying to send "a visible message to the forest."

Deep in the woods, the boy named Crow speaks to Kafka and tells him he must forgive his mother for abandoning him. Kafka must return to the woods—to nature—for this revelation. In the forest he also meets two soldiers, visitors from another time who lead Kafka through a strange entrance to another dimension. One of the soldiers informs Kafka that time is not "a major factor here."

Nature also plays a role in Hoshino's quest to find the entrance stone. Colonel Sanders leads Hoshino to a woody area with a shrine before he reveals that the stone is hidden there. The shrine is Shinto, an Eastern religion with its roots in nature. It is a thunderstorm that finally opens the entrance stone.

Subjective Truth

Reading *Kafka on the Shore* leaves many readers wondering which "facts" are true. Is Miss Saeki really Kafka's mother? Did something supernatural happen when Nakata was a boy? Is Johnnie Walker really the icon from the scotch label—is he even real? As in a number of his books and stories, Murakami leaves many of these questions unanswered, forcing readers to come to their own conclusions.

Kafka's relationship with Miss Saeki is filled with coincidences. In her past she also knew a young man named Kafka, with whom she fell in love. Was that man Kafka's father, and is he Miss Saeki's son? There is no way of knowing the objective truth about these questions. In the cabin deep in the woods, Kafka asks the specter of Miss Saeki directly—"Are you my mother?" She can only answer: "You already know the answer to that." Yet, Kafka says that answer cannot be expressed in words. From a subjective angle, perception replaces factual proof.

On a subjective level, Kafka, by accepting Miss Saeki as his mother, can learn to forgive his mother's abandonment. His interior voice tells him: "Mother, you say. I forgive you. And with those words, audibly, the frozen part of your heart crumbles." This subjective "truth," finally enabling Kafka to move beyond the anger and hurt in his heart, becomes more important than factually proving that Miss Saeki is his mother.

Analysis

Throughout their separate journeys, Kafka and Nakata encounter a number of characters, many of whom seem bizarre or different. Both protagonists attract the help and friendship of many characters—including a transgendered librarian and a classical-music-loving trucker.

Kafka Tamura

Kafka Tamura is a fifteen-year-old runaway who has been abandoned by his mother and cursed by his father. We never learn his real first name, but we recognize the name he has adopted: Kafka, after the Czech writer Franz Kafka, who wrote nightmarish stories about tortured protagonists. As the sole first-person narrator in the double narrative, Kafka becomes the most identifiable character in the novel. An avid reader with an inquisitive mind, he seems highly intelligent for his age.

By running away, Kafka escapes an abusive father in a loveless home. Still, his father's prediction that Kafka would murder him and sleep with his mother (and sister) haunts Kafka throughout the story. He wonders if each woman he meets is either his real mother or sister. This fear and his need to forgive his mother become the true burdens of his travels. Like a character in a fairy tale, Kafka accepts the challenges he encounters on his journey. By doing so, he is befriended by almost everyone who encounters him, including Sakura, Oshima, and Miss Saeki.

Throughout his travels, Kafka is accompanied by an interior voice, the boy named Crow. This voice seems to

Throughout the novel, Kafka is accompanied by a voice that seems to come from Kafka's subconscious. He is called Crow. In the theatrical version of the novel performed by Chicago's Steppenwolf Theatre, he is an actual character who is always with him.

emanate from Kafka's subconscious. Crow speaks to the teenager, particularly at difficult or disturbing times. At times, Crow seems to function as the boy's conscience. Through him, Kafka grows and learns to accept himself.

Murakami comments: "When I wrote *Kafka on the Shore*, I became a fifteen-year-old kid, actually. I could feel like a fifteen-year-old kid, I thought like a fifteen-year-old kid, and I saw the world from the eyes of a fifteen-year-old kid."

Satoru Nakata

A mentally challenged sixty-year-old man who casts a weak shadow, Nakata survives by living off a government subsidy and by locating missing cats. The story of Nakata's inexplicable coma as a child opens the novel and establishes a strange, otherworldly origin for his unique behavior and abilities. He loses all connections to his own memory, establishing him as a character with no real past—one who lives gladly in the present.

Nakata's ability to communicate with cats reinforces both his childlike traits and his connection to nature. "Actually almost all the basic knowledge he had about the world and how it worked he learned from his feline friends." Still, the kind and placid Nakata is forced into bloody action when the eerie figure of Johnnie Walker kills cats in front of the horrified old man. Nakata's act of violence stops Johnnie Walker's slaughter—but afterward, he can no longer talk to cats.

Like Kafka, Nakata attracts the help of almost everyone around him. Truck drivers offer him rides and buy him food, and Hoshino is moved by Nakata's kindness to help the old man on his journey. Nakata does not question his goal of reaching Shikoku. Instead, he lives a life full of acceptance. As he tells Miss Saeki: "Whether it's right or wrong, I accept everything that happens, and that's how I became the person I am now." He also acts as a figure of sacrifice. Referring to his killing of the murderous Johnnie Walker, he tells Miss Saeki that he "took the place of a fifteen-year-old boy who should've been there." If he actually killed Kafka's father in that instance, Nakata has taken on the burden of the crime.

Oshima

The androgynous Oshima offers Kafka the greatest assistance throughout the novel. He immediately befriends Kafka and convinces Miss Saeki to let the fifteen-year-old runaway stay in the library. As they become closer, Oshima becomes a trusted confidant and guide: he prods Kafka intellectually and forces him to realize he must live in his own way. Together, they discuss art, history, literature, and psychology.

Oshima compels Kafka to search for a deeper meaning in life, to see through the obvious. "Everything in life is metaphor," he tells Kafka. When Oshima brings Kafka to his family's mountain cabin in Shikoku, he provides the setting through which Kafka can pass through this world and into another.

Oshima is slender and delicate in appearance, yet his dress indicates to Kafka that he is male. However, Oshima explains: "My body is physically female, but my mind's completely male. . . . Emotionally I live as a man. . . . My sexual preference is for men. . . . I'm a female but I'm gay." Murakami once explained his intention with Oshima's unclear sexuality: "Oshima is by his very nature innocent, lacking any kind of impurity. . . . . Only a person like this could be a guide for Kafka. . . ."

Hoshino

Hoshino, the twenty-something truck driver who befriends Nakata, may be the character closest to the more "typical" Murakami protagonist. His attitudes toward work are noncommittal at best, and he gladly abandons his job to accompany Nakata to Shikoku. Like many Murakami characters, Hoshino has rejected the thought of ever working for a boss in a large company. A lover of classical music, Hoshino is also prone to philosophical musings on the meaning of life.

Hoshino's aloha shirt represents his casual attitude toward life and work. Born into a farming family, he frequently got into trouble in his teens. His background includes abuse: "I've been punched out my whole life—at home, at school, in the SDF—but I survived. Not to brag or anything, but the days I haven't been hit I could count on both hands." Hoshino is also driven to help Nakata partially by memories of his dead grandfather, who had always supported him and whom he never thanked. Following Nakata, Hoshino says, makes him feel he is "exactly" where he belongs; he compares it to following Buddha or Jesus. As he tells Nakata: "I've started to see the world through *your* eyes."

While walking the streets at night, Hoshino meets Colonel Sanders, who leads the truck driver to the Shinto shrine where the entrance stone is hidden. With Hoshino's help, Nakata uses the entrance stone to open a dimensional "warp." After Nakata dies, Hoshino acquires the ability to speak to cats. Also, it is Hoshino who must destroy the evil white creature that slithers out of Nakata's corpse.

Miss Saeki

Miss Saeki appears to exist on two planes: she is the beautiful, middle-aged woman who runs the private library in Takamatsu, and she is the teenage girl who appears at night to Kafka. Her past is as mysterious as her character. A musician and composer, she fell in love with a boy when both were in grade school. As Oshima tells Kafka, they "were like one in body and spirit." After the boy leaves for Tokyo, she composes a beautiful ballad about her love for him and records it in a studio. That song, "Kafka on the Shore," becomes a huge hit in Japan. She also has an oil painting bearing the same name and depicting the young man standing on the shore. After he died when he was only twenty, beaten to death by rioting students in 1970, Miss Saeki never again sang in public.

When Kafka first sees Miss Saeki, he thinks: "She makes a strong impression on me, making me feel wistful and nostalgic. Wouldn't it be great if this were my mother." Rumors surrounding Miss Saeki claim she married and had a child, but no evidence has ever surfaced. As Oshima describes her, she is "a cipher" who "has a wounded heart."

She tells Kafka that as a young girl she wanted to find an "entrance" to another world, and her song mentions an "entrance stone."

A younger version of Miss Saeki sometimes appears as an apparition in the room where Kafka is staying. In the present, she seems to have sex with Kafka in the middle of the night. Finally, she appears to Kafka again in the mountain cabin in the woods. She dies shortly before the end of the novel.

Johnnie Walker and Colonel Sanders

In one of the most imaginative twists to appear in all his works, Murakami employs the marketing icons of Johnnie Walker and Colonel Sanders as characters in *Kafka on the Shore*. Both characters surface at strange intervals in the novel's events. Murakami uses the immediately recognizable commercial icons as nightmarish figures who seem like visitors from another world.

A neighborhood dog leads Nakata to the violent Johnnie Walker, who is dismayed to find that the simple Nakata does not recognize him. Walker is kidnapping innocent cats, including many of Nakata's friends, and in some of the book's most violent scenes, he is slaughtering the cats and eating their hearts. Walker also stores their heads in a freezer. Forced into action by Walker's murderous behavior, Nakata finally grabs a knife and stabs him to death. The novel poses but does not completely answer the question: Was Walker actually Kafka's father?

Walker, or some form of him, appears again later in the

Johnnie Walker, a well-known Scotch, is a violent, terrifying character in *Kafka on the Shore*—a man who kidnaps cats. In this novel we find that all of our familiar icons and thoughts are turned on their heads.

A character named Colonel Sanders, dressed in white like the symbol of American fried chicken, is, in this novel, a Chekhov-quoting pimp.

novel: he carries a bag with a flute made out of the souls of cats. He is attacked repeatedly by the boy named Crow, who pecks out his eyes. Still, he cannot be completely destroyed. As he explains, he is a "soul in transition . . . formless."

While walking the streets of Takamatsu at night, Hoshino meets Colonel Sanders, the Kentucky Fried Chicken icon. Sanders is a pimp who wants to introduce Hoshino to some call girls, but he also knows the location of the entrance stone. Colonel Sanders knows the police are looking for Nakata, and he advises Hoshino to move to an apartment to avoid them. As he explains to Hoshino: "I'm kind of an overseer, supervising something to make sure it fulfills its original role," and "I'm an abstract concept."

Cats

While cats feature prominently in a number of Murakami's books, they have names and even talk in *Kafka on the Shore*. They function mostly as Nakata's friends and helpers. Nakata's ability to converse with cats stems from his unexplained coma as a child; he calls it his "little secret." Afterward, he discovered he could communicate with cats, and as an adult he makes most of his living locating lost felines. His plot initially concerns finding Goma, a cat missing from a local family's home. Other cats, including a bright Siamese named Mimi, lead Nakata to Johnnie Walker's house, where he is killing neighborhood cats to make a flute out of their souls.

After Nakata dies, his ability to converse with cats transfers to Hoshino. A black cat named Toro informs

Hoshino that he must kill the formless being trying to crawl through the opening created by the entrance stone. Toro tells Hoshino that the truck driver has now taken on Nakata's "role."

Symbols and Motifs

Murakami employs a number of recurring motifs and symbols that help to connect the novel's various themes and narratives.

Kafka on the Shore

Murakami's novel shares its title with a song that Miss Saeki wrote and recorded when she was nineteen. The title also refers to an oil painting showing a boy standing by the sea and to Kafka's photograph of himself and his long-lost sister as children on a beach. The lyrics of Miss Saeki's song reflect the novel's events and characters. In the second line, she writes: "I am in a crater that's no more." When Kafka first sees the apparition of young Miss Saeki, he wonders if he has died "and this girl and I have sunk to the bottom of a deep crater lake."

In the second stanza, the lyrics describe a time when "Little fish rain down from the sky." At one point in the novel—just as Nakata predicts—thousands of sardines and mackerel descend from the sky. Soldiers are mentioned as well in that stanza, and Kafka encounters two World War II soldiers in the woods by the mountain cabin. The song also refers to Miss Saeki's boyfriend, who "sits in a chair by the shore," an image recalling both the painting and Kafka's photograph. The Sphinx, another allusion to the Oedipus myth, is mentioned in the third stanza, as is the entrance stone in the fourth. Finally, the girl in the song wears an "azure dress": throughout the novel, Miss Saeki appears frequently in a blue dress.

At the end of the novel, Miss Saeki gives the oil painting to Kafka. She says it was a present from her boyfriend who died, but she adds: "You were there. And I was there beside you, watching you. On the shore, a long time ago."

Blood

Bloody images recur throughout *Kafka on the Shore,* and this motif connects many of the novel's events. When Nakata's teacher takes his class out on a field trip, she at first neglects to tell authorities that she became aroused, which caused her to have an unusual menstrual flow. She hid a bloody towel in the woods, but it was discovered by Nakata—the real reason she repeatedly struck the boy.

The scene in which Johnnie Walker eviscerates and devours cats, and is then brutally stabbed by Nakata, is one of the bloodiest in all of Murakami's works. Ironically, Nakata awakens after the murder with no blood on him, whereas Kafka is covered in blood when he comes to in the field by the shrine. Another bloody, violent scene occurs when the boy named Crow flies down and attacks Johnnie Walker in the forest. When the boy named Crow pecks at his face and head, blood spurts out everywhere.

In a discussion with Kafka, Oshima reveals that he is a hemophiliac: "Once I start bleeding I have to go to the hospital." In his vision at the cabin, when Kafka finally asks Miss Saeki if she is his mother, she pricks herself in the arm with a hairpin. Kafka then licks the blood off her arm, uniting him symbolically with Miss Saeki as a blood relative.

Entrance Stone

The strange entrance stone that Nakata and Hoshino search for functions as an opening to another dimension or alternate world. Although he does not know why he needs to find it, Nakata says only that the stone needs to be "moved." Colonel Sanders leads Hoshino to the stone, which is hidden by a Shinto shrine. Sanders tells Hoshino that the stone is "meaningless" and that "there's nothing sacred or holy about it."

After Hoshino brings the large stone to Nakata, the old man stares at it, rubs it, and mumbles to it. Nakata relates the stone's power to his experience of losing consciousness as a boy during the war: "Because I'm the one who's gone in and come out again." During a storm, Hoshino is able to flip the stone over, but the effort throws him to the floor. Doing so opens the entrance of the stone, but Nakata cannot explain what has happened. Instead, he tells Hoshino: "I'm doing what I'm doing because I *must*."

By instinct, Nakata knows that he can mention the stone to Miss Saeki when they finally meet. She tells Nakata that she has known about the stone for many years; a line about the stone appears in her song, "Kafka on the Shore." Nakata replies that he has opened it "to restore what's here now to the way it *should* be." Through Nakata, the opening of the entrance stone represents the completion of Miss Saeki's life on earth.

Aristophanes—and the Other Half

In one of his many conversations with Kafka, Oshima discusses the concept of the split self, mentioned by Aristophanes in the ancient Greek philosopher Plato's *Symposium*. According to Aristophanes, all people were at one time joined to another person in one of three forms: male/male, male/female, or female/female. Oshima explains, "But then God took a knife and cut everybody in half, right down the middle. So after that the world was divided just into male and female, the upshot being that people spend their time running around trying to locate their missing other half." This motif resurfaces throughout the novel.

Kafka, in addition to searching for his lost mother, also searches for his lost sister. He wonders if Sakura, the girl he meets at the bus station, who lets him stay in her apartment, might be his sister. When Kafka has sexual encounters with Sakura, both in real time and in his dream at the mountain cabin, he attempts to reunite with her—to become "one" again with his lost sister.

According to Oshima, Miss Saeki's childhood lover was also her other half. Like Kafka, he loved reading and lived in the library. Because he died young, she lost that part of herself and has been living a half-life ever since. When she appears as a fifteen-year-old and sleeps with Kafka, she also attempts to reunite with her lost other half, echoing the

Aristophanes myth. Oshima tells Kafka: "Anyone who falls in love is searching for the missing pieces of themselves."

Literary Reception of the Novel

The *New York Times* named *Kafka on the Shore* one of the "10 Best Books of 2005." In 2006, the novel won both the prestigious Franz Kafka Prize and the World Fantasy Award for Best Novel. In 2007, *Kafka on the Shore* also won the International IMPAC Dublin Literary Award. Although its mythic nature and bizarre plot twists baffled some reviewers, the novel received mostly critical acclaim. Reviewing the book in the *New York Times,* Laura Miller observed about Murakami: "while anyone can tell a story that resembles a dream, it is the rare artist, like this one, who can make us feel that we are dreaming it ourselves."

Writing in the *New Yorker,* John Updike called the novel "a real page turner" and "an insistently metaphysical mind-bender." Updike also found "a schematic rigor in [the novel's] execution." Critic Richard Eder, reviewing the book for the *Los Angeles Times,* called it "gay and severe, tender and horrifying." Writing in *Newsweek,* Malcolm Jones found the prose "unflappable, enchanting: hip but companionable, it keeps you coming back for more."

CONCLUSION

"I WRITE *WEIRD* STORIES," Murakami once told an interviewer, in what most would construe as a serious understatement. Characters talk to cats, disappear into walls, take elevators to different worlds, and become possessed by sheep. In an alluring counterpoint to his undeniable weirdness, Murakami's narrators tend to be everyday people facing the everyday challenges of living in the modern world. Perhaps this aspect explains his enormous popularity.

Critics have tried to impose many labels on Murakami, from magic realist to postmodernist, but he is resistant to these names. "I do not care what labels they put on me," he has observed. "I have my own specific way of writing and no other ways." Murakami jokingly refers to his unique style as "sushi noir," a nod to his Japanese heritage and to the American hard-boiled detective stories that first attracted his literary attention.

In both his novels and short stories, Haruki Murakami has created a literary landscape that is truly all his own. Once readers step into this world there is no turning back. Until the release of each new work, they wait anxiously to see what new world Murakami creates next for them.

WORKS
IN ENGLISH

Novels
Pinball, 1973 (1985)
Hear the Wind Sing (1987)
A Wild Sheep Chase (1989)
Hard-Boiled Wonderland and the End of the World (1993)
Dance, Dance, Dance (1994)
The Wind-Up Bird Chronicle (1997)
South of the Border, West of the Sun (1999)
Norwegian Wood (2000)
Sputnik Sweetheart (2001)
Kafka on the Shore (2005)
After Dark (2007)

Short Story Collections
The Elephant Vanishes (1993)
After the Quake (2002)
Vintage Murakami (2004)
Blind Willow, Sleeping Woman (2006)

Nonfiction

Underground: The Tokyo Gas Attack and the Japanese Psyche (2001)
"To Translate and To Be Translated" (2006)
What I Talk About When I Talk About Running (2008)

Filmography

Tony Takitani. With Issei Ogata. Dir. Jun Ichikawa. 2004.

CHRONOLOGY

1949
January 12: Born in Kyoto, Japan, to Chiaki and Miyuki Murakami.

1968
Attends Waseda University as a theater arts major. Shows little interest in school and spends hours reading film scripts. Is present for but does not participate in a number of student uprisings on campus.

1971
Marries Yoko Takahashi, another student at Waseda.

1974
With Yoko, purchases and runs his first bar, Peter Cat jazz club in Tokyo. The bar is named after one of Murakami's old pets.

1977

Moves Peter Cat jazz club to downtown Tokyo.

1978

While attending a baseball game, is struck by realization that he wants to write a novel.

1979

Writes and publishes first novel, *Hear the Wind Sing,* which wins Gunzo New Writer Award in Japan.

1980

Publishes second novel, *Pinball, 1973.* Writes first short story: "A Slow Boat to China."

1981

Sells Peter Cat Bar and devotes himself to writing full-time. Publishes his first translated collection in Japanese, short stories by F. Scott Fitzgerald.

1982

Starts running. Publishes his third novel, *A Wild Sheep Chase.* Novel wins Noma Literary Newcomer's Prize.

1983

Publishes a translation of Raymond Carver's *Where I'm Calling from and Other Stories.*

1984
First visit to the United States.

1985
Publishes *Hard-Boiled Wonderland and the End of the World*. Novel wins Tanizaki Prize that same year.

1986–1989
The Murakamis leave Japan to live in Europe, including Greece and Italy. Murakami writes *Norwegian Wood* while living in Europe.

1987
Publishes *Norwegian Wood*. Within months, the novel sells two million copies in Japan.

1988
Publishes *Dance, Dance, Dance*.

1989
A Wild Sheep Chase becomes Murakami's first novel to be translated for the English-speaking world.

1990–1991
An eight-volume edition of Murakami's writings is published in Japan.

1991–1995

The Murakamis live in the United States. Murakami serves as a visiting scholar at Princeton University in 1992, and as a writer-in-residence at Tufts University from 1993–1995. While at Princeton, researches Japan's involvement in World War II.

1992

South of the Border, West of the Sun is published. Gives the Una's Lecture in the Humanities at the University of California–Berkeley.

1993

The Elephant Vanishes, first English-language collection of short stories, is published.

1994

The Wind-Up Bird Chronicle is published.

1995

The Murakamis return to Japan, shortly after the Kobe earthquake and the Tokyo gas attacks. *The Wind-Up Bird Chronicle* wins the Yomiuri Prize for Literature.

1996

Interviews both victims of the gas attack and members of the cult who carried out the attack.

1997–1998

First volume of *Underground: The Tokyo Gas Attack* is published in 1997; second volume is published the following year.

1999

Sputnik Sweetheart is published. *Underground* wins the Kuwabara Takeo Prize.

2000

After the Quake is published.

2001

In January, the Murakamis move to Oiso, Japan.

2002

Kafka on the Shore is published.

2003

Publishes a Japanese translation of J. D. Salinger's *The Catcher in the Rye*.

2004

Birthday Stories: Selected and Introduced by Haruki Murakami is published by Harvill Press on Murakami's fifty-fifth birthday: January 12. In Japan, a movie is made of Murakami's short story, "Tony Takitani."

2006

Blind Willow, Sleeping Woman, a collection of short stories, is published. *Kafka on the Shore* wins both the Franz Kafka Prize and the World Fantasy Award for Best Novel. *Blind Willow, Sleeping Woman* wins the Frank O'Connor International Short Story Award.

2007

After Dark is published. *Blind Willow, Sleeping Woman* wins the Kiriyama Prize for Fiction from the Pacific Rim Voices Project.

2008

Publishes a memoir: *What I Talk About When I Talk about Running.*

NOTES

Throughout the manuscript, all references to Haruki Murakami's works refer to the following editions:

Pinball, 1973, Kodansha English Library, Tokyo, 1985.

Hear the Wind Sing, Kodansha English Library, Tokyo, 1987.

Hard-Boiled Wonderland and the End of the World, First Vintage International Edition, New York, 1993.

Dance, Dance, Dance, First Vintage International Edition, New York, 1995.

The Wind-Up Bird Chronicle, First Vintage International Edition, New York, 1998.

South of the Border, West of the Sun, First Vintage International Edition, New York, 2000.

Norwegian Wood, Vintage International Original, New York, 2000.

A Wild Sheep Chase, First Vintage International Edition, New York, 2002.

Sputnik Sweetheart, First Vintage International Edition, New York, 2002.

Kafka on the Shore, First Vintage International Edition, New York, 2006.

After Dark, First Edition, Knopf, New York, 2007.

Chapter 1

p. 9, "And it was at that. . . .": Haruki Murakami, *What I Talk About When I Talk About Running,* New York: Knopf, 2008, 27.

p. 10, "My parents. . . .": Richard Williams, "Marathon Man," *Guardian,* May 17, 2003.

p. 10, "I was very influenced. . . .": Jay McInerney, "Roll Over Basho," *New York Times,* September 27, 1992.

p. 11, "That was the first time. . . .": Murakami, "Jazz Messenger," *New York Times,* July 8, 2007.

p. 11, "I didn't study in high school. . . .": Jay Rubin, *Haruki Murakami and the Music of Words,* London: Vintage, 2005, 20.

p. 12, "real live human beings. . . .": Rubin, *Haruki Murakami,* 27.

p. 15, "a young man. . . .": Elizabeth Devereaux, "Japan's Premiere Novelist," *Publisher's Weekly,* September 21, 1991.

p. 15, "Murakami has said. . . .": Rubin, *DLB,* Detroit: Gale Research, 1997, 137.

pp. 20–21, "Translation is a kind of. . . .": Devereaux, *Publisher's Weekly.*

p. 21, "You have to know. . . .": Devereaux, *Publisher's Weekly.*

p. 21, "Many Japanese critics. . . .": Rubin, *Haruki Murakami,* 36.

p. 22, "disposable entertainment,": Rubin, *Haruki Murakami,* 7.

p. 22, "this physical discipline. . . .": Rubin, *Haruki Murakami,* 96.

pp. 26–27, "a bold new advance . . .": *New York Times* reviewer, quoted in promotional material in Murakami, *A Wild Sheep Chase.*

p. 27, "in the topmost ranks. . . .": *Newsday* reviewer quoted in promotional material in Murakami, *A Wild Sheep Chase.*

p. 27, "By writing *A Wild Sheep Chase*. . . .": Rubin, *Haruki Murakami,* 82.

Chapter 2

p. 29, "Raymond Carver was. . . .": Richard Williams, "Marathon Man," *Guardian,* May 17, 2003.

p. 30, "is Murakami's most elaborate. . . .": Jay Rubin, *Haruki Murakami and the Music of Words,* London: Vintage, 2005, 128.

p. 31, "I had never written. . . .": Williams, "Marathon Man," May 17, 2003.

p. 32, "although what Toru narrates. . . .": Janice P. Nimura, "Rubber Souls," *New York Times,* September 24, 2000).

pp. 33–34, "the novel has a relentless pace. . . .": Alexander Harrison, *Times Literary Supplement,* London, quoted in Gale Reference Team, "Biography—Murakami, Haruki (1949–) *Contemporary Authors On-line,* Thomsen Gale, 2007.

p. 34, "but while living in America. . . .": Jay McInerney, "Roll Over Basho: Who Japan is Reading, and Why," *New York Times,* September 27, 1992.

p. 35, "the way in which memory. . . .": Mary Hawthorne, "Love Hurts," *New York Times Book Review,* February 14, 1999.

p. 36, "I want to portray Japanese society. . . .": Rubin, *Haruki Murakami,* 203.

p. 37, "no matter how fantastical. . . .": Jamie James, "East Meets West," *New York Times,* November 2, 1997.

p. 38, "always wanted to apply his. . . .": Ian Buruma, "Becoming Japanese," *New Yorker,* December 23 & 30, 1996, 71.

p. 38, "I thought 1995. . . .": Velisarios Kattoulas, "Pop Master," *Time,* November 17, 2002.

p. 41, "Murakami again displays. . . .": Bruce Tierney, *BookPage,* May 2001.

p. 41, "One of the themes. . . .": Haruki Murakami, talk given at New School, New York, November 3, 2000.

p. 44, "a real page-turner. . . .": John Updike, "Sub-conscious Tunnels," *New Yorker,* January 24, 2005, 91.

p. 47, "a bittersweet novel. . . .": Juvenal Acosta, "A Sleepless Night in Tokyo with Murakami," *San Francisco Chronicle,* May 13, 2007.

Chapter 3

p. 57, "When I write fiction. . . .": Haruki Murakami, interview with the author, May 9, 2008.

p. 57, "Now, what my protagonists. . . .": Velisarios Kattoulas, "Pop Master," *Time,* November 17, 2002.

p. 59, "The subconscious is. . . .": Haruki Murakami, interview by Laura Miller, "The Outsider: Haruki Murakami," *Salon,* December 16, 1997.

p. 59, "Mamiya's narrative. . . .": Matthew Strecher, *Haruki Murakami's* The Wind-Up Bird Chronicle*: A Reader's Guide,* New York: Continuum, 2006, 32.

p. 59, *"The Wind-Up Bird Chronicle* continues. . . .": Jay

Rubin, *Haruki Murakami and the Music of Words,* London: Vintage, 2005, 214.

p. 61, "flow between the conscious. . . .": Strecher, *Haruki Murakami's* The Wind-Up Bird Chronicle, 55.

p. 67, "a metaphor for . . .": Strecher, *Haruki Murakami's* The Wind-Up Bird Chronicle, 61–62.

pp. 68–69, "How can we. . . .": Murakami, interview with author, May 9, 2008.

p. 69, "a new, embryonic. . . .": Strecher, *Haruki Murakami's* The Wind-Up Bird Chronicle, 31.

p. 71, "marks a significant. . . .": Jamie James, "East Meets West," *New York Times,* November 2, 1997.

p. 71, "closure . . .": Michiko Kakutani, "On a Nightmarish Trek through History's Web," *New York Times,* October 31, 1997.

p. 71, "has the easy authority. . . .": Laura Miller, "The Outsider: Haruki Murakami," December 16, 1997.

p. 71, "series of hauntingly. . . .": Pico Iyer, "Tales of the Living Dead," *Time,* November 3, 1997.

p. 71, "Murakami pulls. . . .": Kevin Hunsanger, "Where's the Cat?" *San Francisco Bay Guardian,* October 29, 1997.

p. 71, "the most impressive thing. . . .": Julian Ferraro, "The Mystery in Room 208," *Times Literary Supplement,* May 1, 1998.

Chapter 4

p. 85, "When I wrote. . . .": Haruki Murakami, interview with the author, May 9, 2008.

p. 87, "Oshima is by his. . . .": Jay Rubin, *Haruki Murakami and the Music of Words,* London: Vintage, 2005, 293.

p. 96, "while anyone can. . . .": Laura Miller, "Kafka on the Shore: Reality's Cul-de Sacs," *New York Times Book Review,* February 6, 2005.

p. 96, "a real page turner . . .": John Updike, "Subconscious Tunnels," *New Yorker* 80, January 24, 2005, 91.

p. 96, "gay and severe…": Richard Eder, *Los Angeles Times,* January 23, 2005.

p. 96, "unflappable, enchanting. . . .": Malcolm Jones, "Strange Trip," *Newsweek,* January 24, 2005.

FURTHER INFORMATION

Books

The Japan Foundation. *A Wild Haruki Chase: Reading Murakami around the World.* Berkeley: Stone Bridge Press, 2008.

Rubin, Jay. *Haruki Murakami and the Music of Words.* London: Vintage Books, 2005.

——————-. "Murakami Haruki." *Japanese Fiction Writers Since World War II.* Edited by Van C. Gessel. *Dictionary of Literary Biography.* Vol.182. Detroit: Gale Research, 1997. 135–142.

Strecher, Matthew. *Haruki Murakami's* The Wind-Up Bird Chronicle: *A Reader's Guide.* New York: Continuum, 2006.

Websites

Haruki Murakami
www.murakami.ch/main_4.html
Includes biography, opinion, musical influences on Murakami's works, interviews, a forum, and a picture gallery.

Haruki Murakami
www.randomhouse.com/features/murakami/site.php
Official Random House site includes biography, reviews,
background on *Kafka on the Shore,* a section on translations
and translators, Murakami screen savers, photographs pro-
vided by Murakami, and musical selections.

Haruki Murakami—Exorcising Ghosts
www.exorcising-ghosts.co.uk/index.html
A British site featuring news, synopses of all works in
English, and links to reviews.

BIBLIOGRAPHY

The following is a selection of the material the author found helpful in his research.

Works by Murakami

Murakami, Haruki. *After Dark*. Translated by Jay Rubin. New York: Knopf, 2007.

_____. *After the Quake*. Translated by Jay Rubin. New York: Vintage, 2002.

_____. *Blind Willow, Sleeping Woman*. Translated by Philip Gabriel and Jay Rubin. New York: Knopf, 2006.

_____. *Dance, Dance, Dance*. Translated by Alfred Birnbaum. New York: Vintage, 1995.

_____. *The Elephant Vanishes.* Translated by Alfred Birnbaum and Jay Rubin. New York: Vintage, 1994.

_____. *Hard-Boiled Wonderland and the End of the World.* Translated by Alfred Birnbaum. New York: Vintage, 1993.

_____. *Hear the Wind Sing.* Translated by Alfred Birnbaum. Tokyo: Kodansha, 1987.

_____. "Jazzy Messenger." Translated by Jay Rubin. *New York Times,* July 8, 2007. http://www.nytimes.com/2007/07/08/books/review/Murakami-t.html (accessed March 16, 2008).

_____. *Kafka on the Shore.* Translated by Philip Gabriel. New York: Vintage, 2006.

_____. *Norwegian Wood.* Translated by Jay Rubin. New York: Vintage, 2000.

_____. *Pinball, 1973.* Translated by Alfred Birnbaum. Tokyo: Kodansha, 1985.

_____. "The Running Novelist." Translated by Philip Gabriel. *New Yorker* 83. June 9 & 16, 2008, 72–77.

_____. *South of the Border, West of the Sun.* Translated by Philip Gabriel. New York: Vintage, 2002.

_____. *Sputnik Sweetheart.* Translated by Philip Gabriel. New York: Vintage, 2002.

_____. "To Translate and to Be Translated," in *A Wild Haruki Chase: Reading Murakami Around the World,* 25–30. Berkeley: Stone Bridge Press, 2008.

_____. *Underground.* Translated by Alfred Birnbaum and Philip Gabriel. New York: Vintage, 2001.

_____. *What I Talk About When I Talk About Running.* New York: Knopf, 2008.

_____. *A Wild Sheep Chase.* Translated by Alfred Birnbaum. New York: Vintage, 2002.

_____. *The Wind-Up Bird Chronicle.* Translated by Jay Rubin. New York: Vintage, 1998.

Works about Murakami

Baruma, Ian. "Becoming Japanese." *New Yorker* 71, December 23 & 30, 1996, 60–71.

Devereaux, Elizabeth. "Japan's Premier Novelist Is 'Seeking New Style.'" Interview with Murakami. *Publisher's Weekly,* September 21, 1991. http://www.gbctrans.com/eotw/pubweekly.html (accessed April 7, 2008).

Gale Reference Team. "Biography—Murakami, Haruki (1949–)," in *Contemporary Authors Online.* Thomson Gale, 2007 (accessed April 17, 2008).

The Japan Foundation. *A Wild Haruki Chase: Reading Murakami around the World.* Berkeley: Stone Bridge Press, 2008.

Kattoulas, Velisarios. "Pop Master." Interview with Murakami. *Time,* November 17, 2002. http://www.time.com/time/magazine/article/0,9171,391572,00.html (accessed May 3, 2008).

McInerney, Jay. "Roll Over Basho: Who Japan is Reading, and Why." Interview with Murakami. *New York Times,* September 27, 1992. http://www.nytimes.combooks/01/06/10/specials/murakami-japan.html (accessed February 28, 2008).

Miller, Laura. "The Outsider: Haruki Murakami." Interview with Murakami. *Salon,* December 16, 1997. http://www.salon.com/books/int/1997/12/cov_si_16int.html (accessed April 7, 2008).

Rubin, Jay. *Haruki Murakami and the Music of Words.* London: Vintage, 2005.

_____. "Murakami Haruki," in *Japanese Fiction Writers since World War II*. Edited by Van C. Gessel, 135–142. Detroit: Gale Research, 1997.

Strecher, Matthew. "Beyond 'Pure' Literature: Mimesis, Formula, and the Postmodern in the Fiction of Murakami Haruki," in *Journal of Asian Studies* 57:2. May 1998.

_____. *Haruki Murakami's* The Wind-Up Bird Chronicle: *A Reader's Guide*. New York: Continuum, 2006.

Updike, John. "Subconscious Tunnels." *New Yorker* 80, January 24, 2005, 91–93.

Williams, Richard. "Marathon Man." *Guardian,* May 17, 2003, http://books.guardian.co.uk/print/0,4669858-99930, 00.html (accessed March 2, 2008).

INDEX

Page numbers in **boldface** are illustrations. Proper names of fictional characters or places are shown by (C).

ABOUT THE AUTHOR

MARK MUSSARI is a freelance writer, translator, and editor living in Tucson, Arizona. He received his Ph.D. in Scandinavian Languages and Literature from the University of Washington and taught for a number of years at Villanova University. He is the author of many nonfiction books for Marshall Cavendish Benchmark, including *Othello* and *Shakespeare's Sonnets* in our Shakespeare Explained series, and *Amy Tan* in this series. He has also published academic journal articles, encyclopedia entries, and numerous magazine articles on art, design, and entertainment.